SPOR**BEST**

BOOK & DVD SERIES

FS Books:
Sportsman's Best: Inshore Fishing
Sportsman's Best: Offshore Fishing
Sportsman's Best: Snapper & Grouper
Sportsman's Best: Sailfish
Sportsman's Best: Trout
Sportsman's Best: Redfish
Sportsman's Best: Dolphin
Sportsman's Best: Snook

Sport Fish of Florida
Sport Fish of the Gulf of Mexico
Sport Fish of the Atlantic
Sport Fish of Fresh Water
Sport Fish of the Pacific

Baits, Rigs & Tackle
Annual Fishing Planner
The Angler's Cookbook

Florida Sportsman Magazine
Florida Sportsman Fishing Charts
Lawsticks
Law Boatstickers

Author, Brett Fitzgerald
Edited by Mike Conner and Florida Sportsman staff
Art Director, Drew Wickstrom, Assistant Art Director, Jim Henderson
Illustrations by Joe Suroviec
Copy Edited by Sam Hudson
Photos by Scott Sommerlatte, Pat Ford, SaltyShores.com,
Rick De Paiva, George Gozdz and Florida Sportsman staff

SNOOK

CONTENTS

SB
SPORTSMAN'S BEST
S N O O K

156

174

188

Anglers tend to relate red mangrove shoreline with snook despite the fish's affinity with a wide range of habitat.

Snook on Stage

It's a rare angler who can be casual about the pursuit of snook. Either you are an avid "snooker" or you're not a snook fisher at all.

Centropomus undecimalis is as demanding of attention as a third wife (or husband, for you ladies of experience) and just as likely to be temperamental, unpredictable and difficult to understand. For those with the addiction, snook are the only fish truly worth chasing, and they do so with a single-minded devotion that is almost religious in intensity.

This book can act both as a guide for the novitiate and a reminder for the old priests of the water. Author Brett Fitzgerald, who reportedly has a fishing kayak permanently grafted to his nether regions, has covered snooking both in width and depth, and almost anyone reading this book will come away a better snook angler for it.

It's all here and it's all accurate and thoroughly explained. Most will find the information on the biology of the fish and how the species fits seamlessly into the eco-systems to be both instructive and fascinating. And understanding a bit of the science of the snook will surely make anyone a better snook fisherman.

Understanding tides is central to your success, and for most of us it takes years until we begin to grasp the complexities even of our home bay, never mind strange waters to which we travel to wet a line. This book is worth reading for that chapter, alone. It explains clearly how the moon, the sun, the wind and even the shape of the bottom in the estuaries affect the rise and fall of the water, and consequently the movements and feeding of snook. And the author is generous with his observations on exactly where the fish are likely to be on various phases of the tide, in habitat varying from blackwater mangrove country to oyster bars and grassflat potholes to inlets and beaches of both Florida coasts.

For those who want to master livebait fishing, all the details are here, from finding and catching a half-dozen bait species to keeping them alive, as well as exactly how and where to fish them. Artificials are covered from top to bottom as is the gear to fish them and the boats to fish them from.

The Pro Tips scattered here and there add a final lagniappe; Fitzgerald has fished with many of the top snook anglers in the state, and many of them have generously offered knowledge here that has taken them decades to accumulate.

And of course the author does not ignore conservation of these grand fish we all love so much. He points out that we live in a time when strong fishery rules have done much to bring back the species, but with more of us on the water every day, it is essential that we buy into the ethics of conservative snook fishing, and do our part to preserve the essential habitat that allows the species to thrive today, and for our kids and grandkids now and tomorrow.

—Frank Sargeant, *Florida Sportsman* Contributing Editor

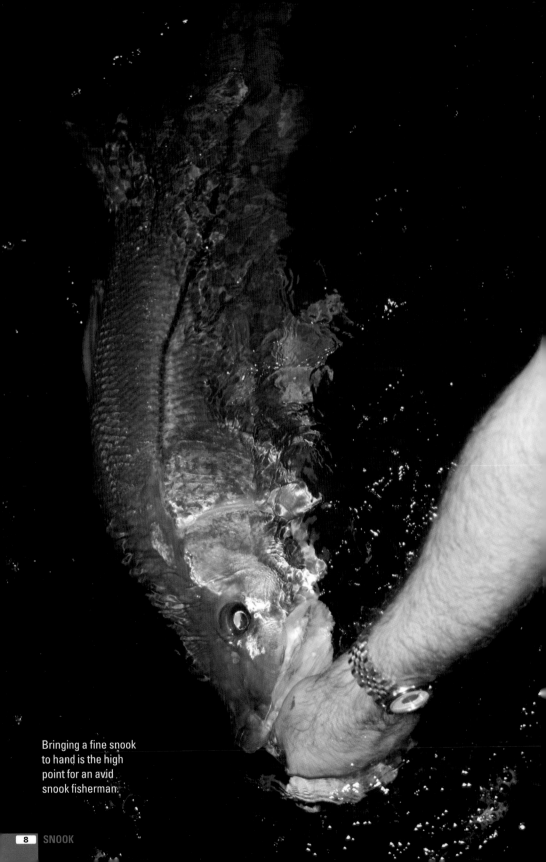

Bringing a fine snook
to hand is the high
point for an avid
snook fisherman.

Introduction

Catch a Shining Star

Among North American saltwater gamefish, snook are a tropical specialty, limited in range to the southern two-thirds of the Florida peninsula and the southern tip of Texas. Water temperature forms a loose boundary, as snook populations will not flourish where the water dips below 60 degrees Fahrenheit for more than a few days at a time.

Within their range, snook are among the most democratic of fish. Few gamefish are as adaptable, habitat-wise. That's largely why anglers of many persuasions hold them in such high esteem. *Centropomus undecimalis*, the common snook, is fair game for any angler, fishing from a boat or afoot, who has the means to get to the coast. Whether you walk the beach, pound the piers and bridges, work the spillways, drift-fish the inlets and passes, sight fish over shallow grassflats, or head for the backcountry, snook will oblige, some of the time, anyway.

Your idea of snooking may be duping a wary fish with a fly in a foot of water under a sun-drenched sky. Or, wrestling a 40-pound monster away from a bridge piling at midnight. You may specialize, or you may mix it up.

There is no right or wrong way to fish for this aggressive predator.

The mullet passes through the valley of the shadow of death…and that death is snook. And the mullet better be afraid.

There is nothing quite like the spectacle of a trophy snook exploding under a wad of hapless baitfish. The carnage is immediate, efficient, and over in a flash. Hook this master of ambush and the fight that follows is likely to include some combination of rodeo-style head shakes; surface-clearing leaps; somersaults; fast, powerful runs; and a dogged determination to get to the nearest structure. In open water, some say the snook is an ordinary fighter. However, in much of this fish's range, line-parting structure such as mangrove roots, oysters and pilings loom. And snook seem to know that freedom is just a short burst away.

All that's assuming you manage to hook one of these maddeningly fickle fish to begin with. Snook anglers must pay close attention to selection of tackle, baits and lures, and to presentations, tides, seasons and other nuances. Those who crack the code come to be known as good, or even expert, snook anglers. Perhaps you know of a local angler with snook prowess. Chances are he or she has paid some dues, put in the time, and punched through that veil of mystique that has long shrouded this fish. At the extreme, the snook's timeless magnetism has caused lost jobs, lost friendships, even broken marriages. But to the addicted snooker, such things aren't all that important anyway.

Snook are most abundant on the Florida Atlantic coast from roughly Flagler Beach south, and the Florida Gulf coast south of Crystal River. In southern Texas, snook are caught from just south of Port Mansfield to the Mexico border. Snook are common in all coastal Central American countries, and along the east coast of South America well into Brazil. Caribbean Islands as close as Cuba and as far away as Trinidad and Tobago are home to snook.

Some offshore anglers take one sip of the snook elixir and never go deep again. For many anglers, the snook is inshore fishing's shining star.

—Brett Fitzgerald

CHAPTER 1

The Fishery

Identifying a fishery, in this case, that of the snook, requires a discussion of the fish's habitat, range and distribution, the anglers, the fish's economic impact, socioeconomic significance and more.

For a fish with such limited range, snook have quite the fan base due to its gamefish qualities primarily, and because it is one of the best on the table. The only U.S. coastal waters that have snook are those of the southern half of Florida and extreme southern Texas. This tropical gamefish is more widely distributed throughout Central America and the Caribbean, where many U.S. anglers flock to target them, or at least include them in their angling itinerary (see Chapter 15, Destinations).

Snook anglers run the gamut. Everyone from live-baiters to fly fishers, fishing from boats or the bank, hold snook in high esteem.

The diversity of anglers after snook is testament to the variety of snook habitat. Each lends to a different expertise, for which specific skills are required.

A golden snook from quiet backcountry waters. Above, the quiet is shattered as a school attacks a school of baitfish.

Snook So Many Ways

The snook is a tropical gamefish whose range in the continental U.S. is basically limited to the lower Florida peninsula with occasional catches made as far north as Crystal River on the Gulf coast, and Fernandina on the Atlantic. Snook also thrive in extreme southern Texas at Port Isabel in the Lower Laguna Madre and are

The fishery is boat-centric . Everything from open fishermen to kayaks qualify.

Snook make a brisk, strong first run and then shorter bursts until brought boatside.

abundant along the entire Mexican coast.

This is a relatively small geographic area, but anglers travel from all over the country to test their skills against this exciting, aggressive gamefish.

So how do you describe the typical snook angler? Sit in on a South Florida fishing club meeting featuring a snook fishing expert as the night's speaker, and you might find a resident "old salt" sitting right next to a "snowbird," each just as skilled within their niche of snook fishing, each happy to teach and learn from the other. You might see a mix of inlet anglers, flats skiff anglers, kayakers,

bridge and pier fishermen, and beach walkers.

The diversity of anglers after snook is testament to the diversity of snook habitat. Each lends to a different kind of expertise, and an angler should develop specific skills. Where and how a snook fisherman goes about it can be looked upon as an extension of personality. A wade-fisherman can walk onto a shallow flat and stroll (or shuffle along, if stingray conscious) to the edge of a flat, and methodically cover every pothole, hump, and bait pod. The same angler can hop in a canoe or kayak and greatly expand his or her range without sacrificing much of that wader stealth, while gaining access to skinny waters or little rivulets that power boats cannot enter.

The snook fishery centers around boats. During the summer, working the big inlets is too dangerous for paddle craft, not to mention pretty difficult due to potentially heavy currents and rough seas. Sometimes snook are concentrated in a very small area, perhaps a particular rivermouth or remote estuarine bay that requires a long run from civilization. In some cases, creative anglers have combined the power and paddle practices to come up with a great way to get to world-class snook waters. Some anglers load kayaks aboard bigger boats for deployment far from the ramp, and combine primitive camping with their snook outings.

Whether you choose to wade, paddle, or hit the inlet in a 26-foot center console boat that doubles as a bluewater fishing machine, you face a plethora of choices as far as technique. Snook anglers fish live bait, dead bait, artificial lures and flies. Some specialize. Some do it all, when the time is right.

Management History

Americans started homesteading South Florida right around the turn of the 20th century. It didn't take long before the human migration made an impact on the snook population. Surprising as it

A snook jumps to shake the hook. Smaller fish jump more frequently, especially in shallow water.

sounds, major declines in numbers were lamented by America's early sportfishermen in the 1930s. In "Big Game Anglers' Paradise," author Moise Kaplan wrote that snook "… used to be easy to find … now more extensive searches are required to locate this fish … unless destructive practices are halted, the snook may be headed for extinction."

Amazingly, that book was published in 1936.

Due in part to declining numbers and diminishing creels, combined with the general opinion that snook had an unpleasant flavor, they fell somewhat out of favor. The unappealing moniker "soap fish" was pinned on the fish, due to the common practice at the time of leaving the skin on the fish for cooking.

But directly following World War II, protein was scarce, and because snook had predictable spawning habits and migration routes, they were extremely easy to find and net in large numbers. For a few years, they provided much-needed protein during very lean times. Even after economic recovery in the late 1940s, tens of thousands of snook were routinely seine netted at several passes. Until netting was banned in Southwest Florida, snook meat was sold for use in cat food for as little as 2.5 cents per pound.

The first size limit for Florida snook was imposed in 1953 (18-inch minimum). In 1957 snook were granted gamefish status and a bag limit of 4 fish, providing further protection. Shortly thereafter, the general consensus was that snook of any size were harder to find in traditionally productive locations.

Everything from runaway pesticide use to unchecked coastal development to gill-netting to hook-and-line poaching was blamed. But by the '80s, inshore fishing had come of age. Boats, tackle, and improved techniques changed the face of fishing, and the snook were back on many an angler's radar screen. Since then, snook stocks have stabilized as a result of intensive research, and stricter limits, tight slot sizes, and longer closed harvest seasons during vulnerable periods in summer and winter.

Although there is not a commercial market for snook, the recreational snook fishery is a very important economic resource to the state of Florida. Today, snook are listed as a "species of special concern." Adding to the complexity of the laws, the east and west coasts of Florida have different

Top, a Florida Everglades backcountry snook on light tackle. Bottom, a 4-fish limit, with only an 18-inch minimum, was once allowed in Florida.

slot sizes and closed seasons. This is because snook on each coast behave differently.

"They are essentially different fisheries," says Ron Taylor, Florida Fish and Wildlife Research Institute (FWRI) scientist. "They spawn differently, feed and grow differently, and anglers approach them with different tactics."

Aside from substantial fishing pressure, snook populations are vulnerable to other factors. Natural phenomena such as extreme cold snaps and red tide can kill thousands of snook at a time. But probably the biggest threat to snook today is habitat loss. By the mid 80s, over half of the mangrove habitat in Florida had been removed.

This habitat is essential for the development of juvenile snook, and the trend of habitat loss is very difficult to reverse. Organizations such as the Snook Foundation have recognized the importance of habitat for all of Florida's gamefish, and are dedicated to protecting and restoring essential habitat. Even so, strict snook fishery management is likely here to stay.

Legislation prohibiting the removal of mangrove trees has been a powerful instrument in preserving Florida's snook population. Anglers are becoming more conscious of this fish's welfare, calling on their fellow anglers to take more personal responsibility when fishing for snook in the closed seasons, and when handling oversize females. Though catch-and-release fishing is not outlawed during closed seasons, many anglers avoid fishing over spawning aggregations in

the inlets and passes. Many who do, avoid using live baits. Many who do use live baits, at least opt for circle hooks to lessen the chance of gut-hooking a fish. Another good practice is supporting a snook's weight by placing a hand under its midsection rather than "hanging" it by the lower jaw when weighing or photographing the fish. There is growing evidence that hanging a heavy snook, or any large fish, by its jaw can damage internal organs. Also, it's wise to release a snook quickly, use sufficient tackle to shorten the fight, and avoid fishing where predators such as porpoises and sharks are known to make quick meals of tired, released snook. SB

Here's a fine snook taken on an an artificial lure in Florida's Indian River Lagoon.

CHAPTER 2

The Snook

Centropomus undecimalis, the common snook, falls into the order Perciformes, or perch-like fishes. The Greek name *Centropomus* means "stinging cover," understandable to dedicated snook fishermen, most of whom have lost a fighting fish, or worse, injured or even lost a finger to the snook's serrated, laser-sharp gill plate. *Undecimalis* refers to fin count—10 spines in the dorsal fin, one of the identifying characteristics of similar species of snook. Also known as robalo, saltwater pike and sergeant fish, the common snook has a complex life history.

Snook have a distinctive, pike-like profile, with a sloping head and protruding lower jaw. Its most recognizable feature is an uninterrupted black lateral line from the top of the gill plate through the fork of the tail. Thus, the popular nickname linesider.

The snook's most recognizable feature is its black lateral line running from the top of the gill plate to the fork of the tail. Thus, the popular nickname linesider.

See DVD for more about snook biology.

Al Barnes
Sight fishing over
backcountry mud flats.

Life History

I n late spring large congregations of adult snook stack up in inlets and passes. On the Florida Atlantic coast, spawning takes place in the major inlets connecting the Atlantic Ocean with the estuarine waters from Cape Canaveral south into Dade County. On the west coast, the major passes will hold spawning snook but a river or

Studies have shown that snook spawning is more dependant on time of day than any particular lunar or tidal phase.

creekmouth might suffice, sometimes deep into an estuary like Tampa Bay.

Spawning in Florida generally starts in April. Males and females will gather and start swimming in a circular direction, forming a spawning "ball." When the time is right, the spawning ball will "erupt." Studies have shown that snook spawning is more dependant on time of day than any particular lunar or tidal phases. Scientists at the Florida Fish and Wildlife Research Institute (FWRI) have demonstrated that current is also a major player in the timing of the release of eggs. Snook can spawn every two or three days throughout the summer, with peak activity in June and August.

Large female snook can release over a million eggs every time they spawn, which can last well into November. This heavy activity requires the females to feed voraciously throughout the summer spawning season, much to the delight of beach anglers fishing the surf closest to an inlet or pass.

Until very recently, it was thought that once a snook found its way to a pass during the spawn, that fish would actively reproduce throughout the season. This led scientists to believe that every female fish was releasing huge numbers of eggs every other day for 150 to 180 days. But acoustic tagging studies have suggested otherwise.

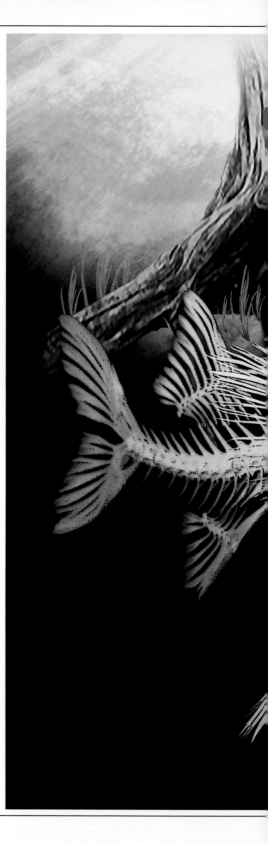

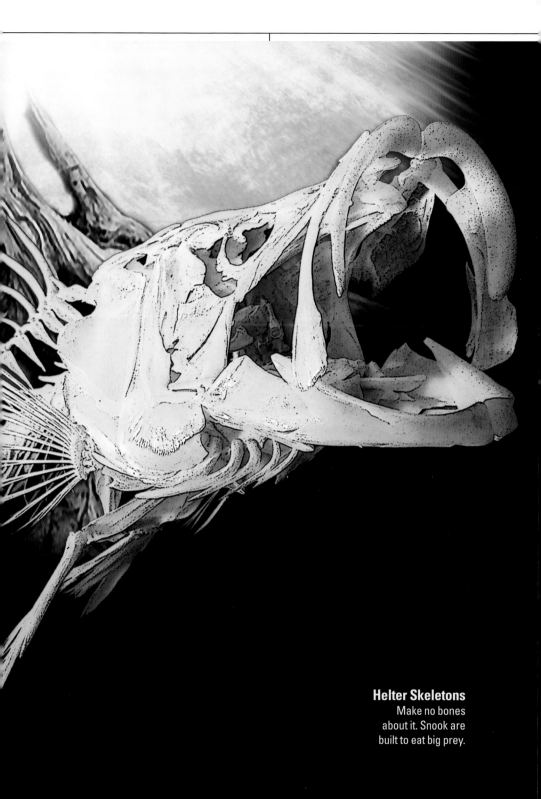

Helter Skeletons
Make no bones
about it. Snook are
built to eat big prey.

Joe Suroviec
Snook and pilchards
in the mangroves.

First, while it is clear that most snook return to the same inlet or pass every year to spawn, they don't necessarily show up at the first sign of spawning activity, nor do they always stay until the final round. In other words, while some fish might start spawning in April at a given site, not

While some snook start spawning in April at a given site, not every fish with an invitation shows up for the opening act.

every fish holding an invitation shows up for the opening act. For a percentage of snook, spawning may take place over a shorter period of time than originally suspected.

Scientists also believed that snook would spawn roughly every other day while at the spawning site. But now they think some tagged fish skip out on spawning sessions, possibly decreasing the

spawning of an individual fish by 30 percent or more. So not only are fish not staying at the party as long as once thought, but they are not getting on the dance floor as frequently, either. In fact, some snook never spawn at all. Otolith studies of captured snook show that some fish will even avoid salt water for years at a time, staying in the extreme upper estuaries. Ultimately, it appears that relative to the overall population, the size of each spawning event is 50 percent smaller than scientists originally estimated.

A fertilized egg, or zygote, travels passively with the tides and currents for 12 to 24 hours. The initial release of eggs frequently occurs during an outgoing tide. Some ride the tide into the inlet. Some are carried to adjacent inlets before they slip back inside the estuary. Scientists believe this helps protect the gene pool by avoiding total reproductive homogeny. After a day or so, the zygote will hatch into a larval form. This little critter still is a passive traveler on the current, but can move vertically in the water column. During the day, probably to avoid

Kevin Brant
Snook are "up-feeders" thanks to high-placed eyes.

Pasta Pantaleo
A snook rushes a
school of pinfish.

predation, the larvae drop lower in the water column which slows their rate of drift. In the evening, they rise back up and catch the faster waters. Within days, or a couple of weeks, some of these larvae find their way to their first home,

At about 45 days, the snook is almost two inches long and recognizable and seeks more saline waters.

or habitat, primarily estuarine headwaters. For 35 to 45 days, the minuscule critter will feed on micro-crustaceans. The amount of prey is critical at this stage, and for robust recruitment of any given class of snook, prey must be small enough to fit into a tiny snook's mouth.

By the time the snook is 4 millimeters long, it starts to develop pigmentation cells that give it some color, and by 7 millimeters skeletal development begins. At about 45 days, the snook is almost two inches long and recognizable, and seeks out water with 5 to 15 ppm (parts per million) salinity. Here, the diet switches to small fishes, such as mosquitofish. According to Ron Taylor, lead snook biologist at FWRI, low salinity, low wave energy, warm, fresh water and abundant prey fishes are ingredients for the most important habitat in the snook's life cycle.

Snook reside in sheltered backwaters from about two months to age one, reaching 7 or 8 inches in length. At this point, most of the fish are males, sexually mature and start heading toward the salt. However some will head for fresh water. Scientists have documented snook as old as 8 years that have never left fresh water, and thus have never spawned (salt water is needed to activate the sperm of snook).

For the first couple of years, snook tend to school by size, and for good reason. If a yearling snook were to move into a pass where several hundred huge snook were preparing to spawn, he would likely become prey for an older cousin.

Mark Johnson
Snook closes in on the real thing and an imposter.

Guy Harvey
Linesiders compete
in the buffet line.

Snook are thought of as non-migratory, but females may travel considerable distances from fresh water to open sea.

But as a group, the majority of snook do follow a consistent pattern. During the summer, adult snook are normally at the inlets and passes, or adjacent beaches or reefs. Fall is generally a transition period, as many adult snook make their way deep into the estuary. Some will find suitable habitat along the way and stop. Most will continue on, and will find the deep holes in the rivers or back

Jim Roberts
Traditional Gyotaku
Japanese fish print.

Adult Habitat

While snook are generally thought of as non-migratory, females may travel considerable distances from freshwater rivers to the open sea. Along the way, a snook may hold and feed in deep river channels, along mangrove shorelines, over grassflats and oyster bars, in passes and inlets, and around manmade structures such as pilings, docks and seawalls. There are a few habitats that snook use primarily as grocery stores, probably not taking up residence but hunting for a quick meal. Beaches near spawning congregations and spillways come to mind as examples.

Schools of snook have been found off southeast Florida on reefs more than 60 feet deep. How long they remain there is a mystery, but they are feeding. Plenty of shocked snapper and grouper fishermen will attest to that.

This scenario obviously debunks the belief that snook stay in one estuary for life. In fact, on the east coast, snook tagged with acoustic "ping" tags have been tracked moving north and south, some passing through several separate estuarine systems.

of the estuary to hold up over winter. Spring sees a reverse mini-migration back to the passes.

As snook are intolerant of cold water, no doubt some of this movement within a relatively small ecosystem is related to weather. The deeper holes are less affected by daily fluctuations in air temperature. But this move might also serve to protect snook from some predators, primarily sharks and porpoises. Also, they are likely following bait migrations throughout the estuary.

Predators

In the underwater world, there is a general rule of survival: If it swims and can fit into a bigger critter's mouth, it is probably prey. Thus larval snook are a meal for just about anything that can see them. Juvenile snook wouldn't stand much chance if they stayed in the inlets where their parents consummated their relationship. This is why the shallow, generally fresh water that is directly adjacent to estuaries is so critical for the survival of all species of snook. Shallow water with lots of cover (and smaller prey for snook) is essential.

Brian Sylvester
The predator pins
prey behind bars.

Less Common Snook

I n the continental U.S., the **common snook** rules the roost. No other member of the *Centropomus* family is as plentiful, grows nearly as large or tolerates cool water. That explains the common snook's larger range. Since individual snook tend to remain close to one estuary, common snook on the Florida Atlantic coast are genetically different than Florida Gulf coast snook. They are still close enough to interbreed, and in some cases they probably do.

Less common snook share with common snook a solid, prominent black lateral line.

But the differences are large enough that biologists can tell which Florida coast a fish came from based on a few tests.

What of other snook species? They share with common snook a solid, prominent black lateral line that runs the entire length of their bodies. The subspecies discussed below are even more averse than C. *undecimalis* to leaving their home system. This might be because they have less tolerance for exposure to high-salinity waters.

The **fat snook**, *Centropomus parallelus*, is the closest to the common snook in maximum size. The biggest specimens only rarely reach the lower end of Florida's slot limit, 28 to 32 (or 33, on the Gulf side) inches. The majority of fat snook are caught around structure at night, such as lighted bridges and docks, fooled by small flies that imitate shrimp or other tiny critters drawn to the light. They're more football-shaped than the sleeker common snook.

The IGFA world record for fat snook is under 10 pounds. They are found on both coasts of Florida, in southern Texas, and at various points around the Caribbean down to Brazil. The Loxahatchee River system in Palm Beach County,

Klaus Schuler
"Old Rosie" is the original Roosevelt Bridge on the St. Lucie River in Stuart, Florida. Common, fat, swordspine and tarpon snook can be caught here.

Florida is "fat snook central."

Very recently, a closer look at Florida's fat snook identified a lookalike, the large-scale fat snook. The difference is found by counting the number of scales along the lateral line. Scaled fish do not increase the number of scales throughout their life; the scales simply grow as the fish does. As juveniles, fat snook have been observed demonstrating "aggres-

Common snook

Fat snook

Swordspine snook

Tarpon snook

blend in with a school of like-size mojarra, sneaking in closer to other unalarmed prey to pick off an easy meal.

The **tarpon snook** inhabits many of the same waters as fat snook. As the name implies, the tarpon snook's lower jaw protrudes even more than that of a common snook. Tarpon snook have seven anal fin rays, one more than any other species of snook. The world record tarpon snook weighed less than three pounds. They are frequently caught in totally fresh water.

The **swordspine snook** is the smallest and rarest snook in North American waters. It's found much closer to the freshwater barrier in estuaries than all of its larger cousins. The name is derived from the much longer second anal fin, a dead giveaway for this species. They are fully grown at 12 inches. Their biggest threat to survival is rapidly declining coastal habitat, especially in their Florida range.

Among snook species south of the border, the Mexican snook, *Centropomus poeyi*, is so similar to common snook that the only way to tell the difference is by counting fin rays, gill rakers and scales. They can reach 40 inches and range from the Mexican Gulf coast through Brazil, as well as the islands of Cuba, Jamaica, Haiti and a few others.

The longspine snook, *Centropomus armatus*, is the Pacific version of the swordspine snook. It shares the distinctive long anal spine and is very close in size and shape. It ranges along the Pacific coast from Mexico to Ecuador. Another Pacific strain, the little snook, *Centropomus robalito*, also resembles the swordspine but is even smaller in size, and ranges from Mexico to Panama.

sive mimicry," a practice not yet seen in common snook. Young fat snook have a distinctive black spot behind the dorsal fin, similar to mojarra, a non-predatory fish that might not signal a flight reflex in some smaller fish. Fat snook have been known to

Along the tropical Pacific coast, the two most significant snook species are the white snook, *Centropomus viridis*, and the black snook, *Centro-*

pomus nigrescens. Their range overlaps, from Baja and the Gulf of California to Paita, Peru. Both grow large, with the slightly larger black snook reaching 50 pounds. The pigmentation of black snook is generally more responsive to environment, leading to a darker back in most conditions. But the only true way to tell the difference between these fish is to count the dorsal fin rays. Black snook have nine, white have 10.

Snook do have distant relatives around the world, suggesting the family tree has roots back to when the earth was covered by a single land mass, Pangea. In Africa, the Nile perch (*Lates niloticus*) is a freshwater cousin of the snook family, and is sometimes sold in the U.S. as Lake Victoria snook, contravening federal fish-labeling guidelines. This fish is a beast. When conditions are right, this perch can reach 500 pounds. Nile perch are wicked predators, but not indigenous to the entire continent of Africa. In fact, about 50 years ago, it was introduced to Lake Victoria, which is the second largest freshwater lake in the world. A massive international fishery has since developed, and now hundreds of tons of erroneously labeled African snook are exported each year, but at a price. The general consensus is that somewhere around 200 species of benthic life have been wiped out of the lake since the introduction of the snook-like Nile perch. Some of those fish were found only in Lake Victoria and therefore are now extinct.

In Australia, the barramundi is the most "snook-like" fish outside of the Americas. Barramundi inhabit the same coastal areas, use similar habitats at different points in their life cycle, and feed much the same way as snook.

They spawn at the mouths of estuarine systems and follow similar seasonal movement patterns. Like snook, barramundi are protandric hermaphrodites, having the potential to change sex from male to female. This fish's eyes are located in a similar position to the snook, angling slightly up which lends well to ambush-style hunting. The mouth of the barra looks smaller than a snook, but their jaw has a slightly different "hinge" that allows it to open wider than one might think, for the speedy inhalation of relatively large prey. **SB**

Jason Mathias
Pass snook await the tide change.

CHAPTER 3

Snook Tackle

No snook fisherman can be expected to limit him or herself to one rod. There are too many disparate snook fisheries, or shall we say, snook holes, to handle efficiently with one stick. An angler who goes into a tackle shop looking for that perfect snook rod may have the beach in mind. That would call for one type of outfit, whereas another has plans to head to the jetty or bridge to wrestle with a monster, which would call for an entirely different rod and reel. In fact, well-rounded snook fishermen tend to outfit themselves for every snook fishing scenario under the sun or moon. That means a tackle closet or rod rack with spinning or casting outfits in the 8-pound class for light lures to 25-pound meatsticks for live-baiting. Even 4/0 boat rods have their place, as do fly rods for flats, bridge and docklight fishing.

SNOOK

See DVD for more on snook tackle.

Above, kayak anglers chose spinning tackle to present light lures. Right, fly tackle is ideal in some snook fisheries.

The Whole Arsenal

As covered in Chapter 1, the snook fishery comprises many inshore habitats, calling for snook anglers to master a variety of fishing gear.

For many snook anglers, spinning gear gets the nod. It's great for beginners, but also excels when casting light, soft plastics into tight cover or small live baits into snook holes. For chucking heavy plugs or topwater lures, quite a few anglers prefer a baitcasting (plug) outfit. A medium to medium-heavy casting outfit can provide the leverage required to pull a lunker out of heavy structure. In practiced hands, baitcasting tackle is deadly accurate. Casting gear is also ideal for trolling big plugs or soaking especially big live baits that attract overslot snook. Finally, fly tackle is tremendous for repeated casting to structure or shorelines. When snook target tiny prey, only the fly fisher can match the hatch to get the job done. Docklight snook is the prime example.

Snook will test your tackle from your rod and reel all the way to your knot and hook. If your line isn't wrapped around some kind of structure, the razor-sharp gill plates can still slice through any leader or line that doesn't measure up. Even in open water, the brute strength of a snook will test your knot-tying skills. And if you don't keep busy with at least basic maintenance of your reels and tackle, you might be making a trip to a tackle shop on the way home from a disappointing snook trip.

Angler sets the hook with casting gear. Casting to shoreline cover can be done with either casting or spinning tackle.

Snook will test not only your skills, but every component of your fishing tackle. That includes your rod, reel drag, fishing line, line-to-leader and leader-to-hook connections.

Spinning Tackle

Spinning reels for salt water feature aluminum or graphite bodies, stainless bearings and anti-twist bail rollers.

For many of us, our first spinning outfit marked the end of fishing with kids' gear (think a Snoopy rod) and the move up to the big leagues. Today's spinning reels suited for salt water are in no way like the reels available just 10 to 20 years ago. With markedly improved design, including non-corrosive materials and encased guts for fantastic durability, spinning reels are now the end of the learning curve for many anglers.

One significant recent change is the size of spools. Some oversize spinning reel spools are so huge they look cartoonish compared to the comparatively minuscule gear box. Large spools are designed to cast line with less friction, demanding less angler effort. Additionally, these reels can handle larger-diameter lines without sacrificing capacity. Thanks to the larger spool diameter, an angler can pick up more line with each turn of the handle. Other spinning reel innovations for saltwater use include super-light aluminum or graphite bodies, improved stainless steel ball bearings, synthetic washers and anti-twist bail rollers.

A stout, fast-action spinning rod, top, has power in the butt to land a sizable snook, bottom, in short order.

Gear ratio warrants some consideration when selecting a spinning reel for snook, but not much. Higher ratio means maximum line pickup, but unless you are fishing for snook in some extreme circumstances (such as working artificial lures in an extremely fast tide), speed might not be that important. Since all but the biggest snook aren't likely to go on super long runs, line capacity is not as important as line control. Immediate, effective response to the slightest turn of the handle can help with the "big girls."

If there's a mechanical culprit when a good snook is lost, it's usually a poor—or poorly maintained—drag. A smooth, durable drag might be the most important consideration when choosing between two equal size spinning reels. Front-spool drag assemblies and adjustment knobs are far superior to so-called rear drags. Jerky, sticky drag systems can cause line breakage or pulled hooks at any point during a battle with a large snook.

Anglers preferring
light to medium
spinning tackle can
load them with poly
braid or monofilament
and cast the lightest
lures with ease.

Spinning Rods

Step onto a veteran snooker's boat and you will probably see both conventional and spinning rods. Almost without exception, the spinners are

Angler fights a snook correctly from the butt rather than high-sticking with the tip.

www.prolite

from 6 inches to as much as two feet longer, with a softer action (more flex). Spinning rods between 7 and 8 feet long cover the bases for snook fishing. Excluding the stiffest of "broomsticks" designed specifically for live baits, most spin rods allow you to cast a light lure. For skipping soft-plastic baits under mangroves or on the flats, a medium-soft tip is probably the best choice. Compared to conventional rods, spinning rods have larger diameter guides to allow for passage of the spirals of line off a spinning reel spool. Spinning rods typically have softer tips than conventional rods.

Picking a rod for your reel boils down to personal preference and whichever habitat you decide to fish for snook. You could follow the manufacturer's line-test and lure-weight ratings on the rod blank (though many have very wide ranges such as 8- to 17-pound-test line) to select a reel for the outfit. Or, just go by feel—the combo should be balanced in your hand, and not too "reel heavy" or "rod heavy." Many anglers pick the smallest, lightest spin reel available with adequate capability and capacity to handle a particular pound-test line for the rod.

Deciphering Fishing Rod Action and Power

Fast

Medium/fast

Medium

The three basic actions of fishing rods. Most manufacturers list action and power ratings in print or online.

Manufacturers frequently describe a rod's character with the words power or action. Power refers to the strength of a rod. Finished rod labels have words like heavy, medium-heavy, medium and so on.

Action refers to how much, and where, the rod bends when a load, or resistance, is applied. Action is described by terms such as fast, medium/fast or moderate/fast. Basically, the slower the rod the

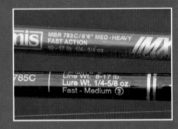

more it bends farther down the blank. For example, a medium-action rod would be better suited for lobbing soft-mouthed live baits than a fast rod. Unfortunately, power and action are not universally defined across manufacturers. Further, other words are frequently substituted, such as taper. A rod that tapers down quickly near the tip typically has a fast action. Construction materials provide clues about a rod's nature. A pure graphite rod or a composite that contains some glass will normally be light and faster in action than a like-size fiberglass rod . SB

Spinning rod rear and foregrips can be cork or synthetic, solid or segmented, and come in a variety of lengths.

Baitcasting Tackle

The fear of backlashing has been tempered by the advent of friction, magnetic and variable weight braking systems.

Conventional (baitcasting/plug) tackle has been favored by anglers targeting big snook for decades. There are serious snook anglers prowling docks and bridges in hundred-dollar johnboats brimming with thousands of dollars worth of stout plug rods. It's just hard to beat the old-fashioned, "round" high-power reels for landing monster snook.

Conversely, when snook fishing along mangrove shorelines, docks, or seawalls with topwater plugs, a low-profile "bass-style" plug reel probably makes the most sense. Snook in those fisheries seldom run as large; plus, most low-profile baitcasters can handle light line and lures better than the round reels. Before buying a low-profile reel, determine whether it is designed for salt water, or be fastidious about clean-up and maintenance. If not, it probably won't last more than a season or two.

Low-profile reels are ideal for casting plugs. Below, mangrove shoreline snook.

In the big-snook game, the round baitcasting reels generally get the nod for trolling big diving plugs in rivers and canals, working spillways with oversize jigs such as Flare Hawks, soaking big live mullet from bridges, or drifting big baits in passes and inlets.

The fear of casting backlashes has been tempered somewhat in recent years thanks to the advent of friction, magnetic and variable-weight braking systems. By design, the leverage provided by the "reel-on-top" plug rods surpasses that of a spinning outfit. Baitcasting rods are generally stiffer, giving the angler an obvious leg up in the power department. The smaller guides complement the design of the revolving spool, allowing fishing line to travel straighter off the spool. With the ability to thumb the spool, you can both control the precise distance of a cast, and apply additional drag pressure once you have hooked up.

Round baitcasting reels
(left) and lighter low-profile
casting reels (right).

Baitcasting Rods

The differences between spinning and baitcasting rods are readily apparent. One, the guides are smaller on average; the line comes off a baitcasting reel straight rather than in coils as it does off a spinning reel spool. Most baitcasting rods are stiffer on average, though there are 7-foot-plus rods with soft tips for lighter lures. The grip has a "pistol trigger" for your forefinger. The shortest rods (in the 6-foot range) tend to have short rear grips so that an angler can cast one-handed, and hold the rod with the reel closer to the body while fishing a lure or fighting a fish. The heaviest rods are generally preferred by those after big snook.

Most baitcasting rods are stiffer on average from butt to tip than spinning rods.

Prevent Those Backlashes

A backlash occurs when the reel spool revolves faster (thus paying out more line) than a lure is pulling out on its flight to a target. The key to preventing backlashes is slowing the spool down with a combination of thumb friction and whatever casting-control features the reel provides.

Most reels have a friction knob on the sideplate

A basic magnetic cast control slows the spool.

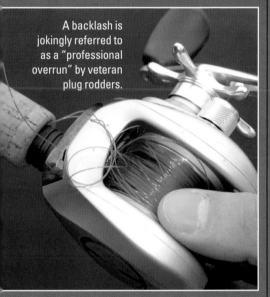

A backlash is jokingly referred to as a "professional overrun" by veteran plug rodders.

At the very least, adjust the friction-control knob.

that slows the reel spool to varying degrees. Higher-end models now come with centrifugal braking systems that allow you to adjust small pins to fine-tune the speed of the spool. With this system, you can tweak the reel ever so slightly to accommodate a wide range of lure weights.

But it's best to use your thumb primarily to apply friction to the spool. You will quickly discover that the worst "bird's nests" form if you fail to stop the reel spool as the lure hits the water. They also form at the start of the cast if you overpower it , especially with a relatively light lure. Get in the habit of thumbing the spool a bit more when casting into a headwind, which slows the lure appreciably. The goal is to prevent backlashes without cutting casting distance too much. SB

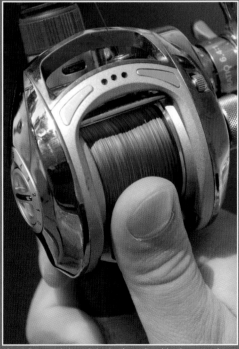
An educated thumb is the best backlash control.

Fly Tackle

Fly fishing for snook is a tale of two fisheries, literally as different from each other as night and day. Probably the most publicized snook fly fishing of all is practiced after the sun goes down, working lighted docks and bridges. However, fly fishing is practicable from the surf to the interior of the estuaries, and that includes shallow flats where sight fishing is the drill.

Snook fishermen looking for ideal fly rods should first consider the sizes and types of flies they will cast most. Size of the fish is of secondary importance, but does have a bearing on rod choice. Also, the fish's proximity to structure must be considered. For instance, you can certainly cast a small minnow fly at a dock light with a 6-weight fly rod. But is that enough rod to horse that 10-pounder that crashes the party where 3-pounders are feeding?

A 6- or 7-weight rod should be considered an ultralight, 8- and 9-weights are middle weights, and 10-weights and greater are reserved for big

Snook fishermen looking for the ideal flyrod weight should first consider

flies and poppers, and big snook. Most anglers fish 9-foot rods; however, shorter rods have their place in tight quarters and are less tiring to cast for hours on end. Combing a mangrove shoreline with air-resistant hair bugs and poppers is a perfect example of short-rod work. In practiced hands, a sub-9-footer delivers tight loops, and depending on the rod's overall stiffness and taper, is a superior fighting stick. This kind of rod excels for docklight and bridge fishing, too, because casts are generally short. In the case of docks, an 8-foot rod can deliver tight loops while casting sidearm.

Fly tackle has grown in popularity with anglers who wade-fish or sight cast from boats, opposite.

the size and weight of the flies they cast the most.

Below, from left to right, 9-weight outfits loaded with intermediate sinking, clear floating and traditional PVC floating line. Most snook fishing can be covered with these lines.

On the opposite side of the spectrum, a growing cadre of beach fly anglers are turning to spey rods, or so-called two-hand rods. They excel for long-distance casting, designed specifically to increase line speed. These rods are generally 9- through

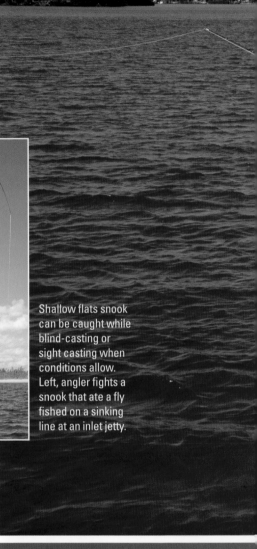

Shallow flats snook can be caught while blind-casting or sight casting when conditions allow. Left, angler fights a snook that ate a fly fished on a sinking line at an inlet jetty.

12-weights, ranging from 11 to 14 feet long. They allow casters to shoot big streamers out over the breaking waves when snook are running in the second trough parallel to shore, or on the far side of nearshore hardbottom reefs, one of the great summer snook magnets. Of course, it's common for snook to cruise right against the sand, well within reach of a 9-foot rod.

Most fly fishers eventually take a liking to fast-action fly rods—they generate maximum line speed which translates to distance for casters with proper form. A fast-action rod tapers dramatically in the upper quarter of the blank; it flexes closer to the tip, recovers (straightens) faster, generally allowing for tighter casting loops. But many beginners find they cast better with a slower action rod, something that flexes a bit deeper in the blank. Manufacturers use terms such as medium-fast; for example The Orvis Company uses the term mid-flex to rate their medium-fast action rods, and tip-flex for their fastest rods. There is a rod action available for all casting styles.

Fly Reels

A fly reel's primary purpose is to hold fly line and backing. A simple click-drag reel used in fresh water will certainly handle small snook. Just enough drag pressure to prevent overrun, with perhaps a little palming by the angler is all that's called for when a snook makes a short run. However, when a big fish thumps your fly, you are better served by a reel with a decent disc drag, and perhaps a large arbor design that allows you to retrieve line as fast as possible when a hot fish doubles back and runs toward you. SB

Large arbor reels are popular primarily because they allow for fast line pickup.

Fishing Lines

There are ideal snook-fishing applications for both monofilament and gel-spun polyethylene.

The variety of lines available today is staggering, and beyond a few generalizations, the choice of which brand you choose to snook fish becomes as much a point of personal prefer-

Both monofilaments and gel-spun polyethylene line come in many colors.

ence as anything. From standard monofilament to gel-spun polyethylene (so-called braid) to the newer hybrids, there is no shortage of choice, and there are ideal snook-fishing applications for each.

Monofilament

For versatility compared to price point, monofilament is tough to beat. Younger snook anglers might say mono slices too easily to catch big snook. Oldtimers will think differently. It can be

used with spin or plug tackle, comes in a variety of colors, and is manufactured in a wide range of limpness, abrasion resistance and stretch.

All mono line stretches, which can either improve or hinder your snook fishing. While it might not help you walk the dog, straight-swimming crankbaits will track smoother (less jerky) than with non-stretch lines. Stretch will sacrifice some control while battling a frisky snook, but might improve the hookset for the jumpy angler who is fishing small baits. Of course, the amount of stretch is relative to the length of line between your lure and your reel. At close range, stretch might not be a player in the hookset or fight. However, there will be a point when too much line is out, allowing for too much stretch to muscle any kind of hookset no matter how violently the angler rears back.

Most monofilament lines float high on the water, a consideration when selecting a leader material for different applications. For heavy jigs, it might not matter at all, but with a small popping bug or deer-hair fly (a deadly mangrove snook material) mono might be the only logical choice.

Nylon copolymers and nylon/fluorocarbon lines

are also available, with different diameter-strength ratios, stretch characteristics and other qualities.

Poly Braids and Hybrids

Polyethylene lines in several manifestations can be a perfect match for snook fishing when traditional nylon monofilament is not the optimal choice.

A gelspun line is basically strands of polyethylene braided or fused into one thread. Some manufacturers will add silicone, Teflon or other compounds along the finishing process, but for the most part the general idea is the same.

Gelspun braid lines come with two distinct differences from mono that attract a lot of snook anglers. First, the diameter is much smaller than mono at the same tensile strength. Most 20-pound braids are equal in diameter to 6-pound monofilament. That translates into greater casting distance as well as capacity on the reel.

The second major plus of braided line is the lack of stretch. The sensitivity compared to mono is far superior, and every yard of line out makes this difference even more glaring. An example of the perfect application of non-stretching lines is when feeling for the sometimes maddeningly subtle strike while drifting live baits or working jigs.

Third, the gelspun lines seem immune to the twist factor that dogs novice spinning reel anglers.

There are reasons that braid has not completely taken over the snook angler's market. First off, per yard, it is generally about six times as expensive as mono. Second, if spooled with too little tension or casting into wind, unmanageable knots can appear during the cast, making the entire fishing rig useless until respooled or the line is cut behind the undesired knot. Finally, the lack of stretch just doesn't make every angler comfortable in every application.

Key Knots for Braid

Most snook anglers use braid, period. But since most anglers cut their teeth on monofilament, many are using knots that are not best suited for braided lines. Here are two that will get you through just about any snooky scenario:

Bimini twist. If you are serious about fishing, it's time to buckle down and learn this knot, which should be used when doubling your braid before tying it to a leader. I believe inferior "line doubling" knots are responsible for just as many lost snook as the legendary gill plates. A Surgeon's loop is frequently substituted, but with no stretch, braid can cause a weak point where the small loop knot constricts the main line, and a strong head shake can cause the unthinkable.

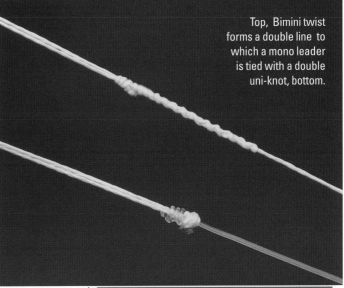

Top, Bimini twist forms a double line to which a mono leader is tied with a double uni-knot, bottom.

Double Uni-knot. When your doubled braid is attached to any diameter leader, be it mono or fluorocarbon, the double uni will suffice. Remember, if the leader is very heavy only 3 turns are required. And after you tie a Bimini into your braid first, a well tied uni-knot simply will not fail. SB

Fly Lines

Snook can be caught on flies anywhere from the surface to depths up to 20 feet or even more. Therefore, floating, intermediate (very slow sink rate) sink-tip and full sinking lines (with varying sink rates) all have their place. All fly lines designed for salt water are weight-forward in design. Tapers can vary; just remember that the head (front 30- to 45-foot section closest to the fly) of the line must be outside the rodtip to load the rod and carry the lighter-weight, smaller-diameter shooting section through the guides. The shorter the head the more weight (expressed in grains) concentrated up front. So-called saltwater tapers (once called "bassbug" taper) have short heads that excel for short casting with big flies. For long casts, you'll need to carry more line in the air, so choose a standard floating line that has a longer head. Most floating lines have "balloons" of air in their plastic (PVC) coating (though there are some polyurethane coatings on the market now) to keep them afloat. Floating lines should be cleaned regularly; dirt and algae can make them sink in the surface layer and make them harder to shoot through the guides. Fly lines are labeled to designate the fact they are weight-forward, the ideal rod weight to match with, and whether they float or sink. For example, a weight-forward, 9-weight floating line packaging would be labeled: WF-9-F. The common cores of floating lines include braided nylon, braided monofilament and single-strand monofilament. The former core is the limpest, the latter the stiffest. Monofilament cores are best in hot weather, thereby snook country. They result in a stiffer line in the heat that shoots well through the guides, though do have more memory in cold

> ## Cores of floating lines can be made of braided nylon, braided monofilament or single-strand monofilament.

Left to right, floating, clear intermediate, medium-sinking and fast-sinking lines. The darker the sinking line, the faster it sinks.

water, so needs extra stretching.

Full-sinking lines sink at different rates, depending on how much tungsten is added to the coating. Most modern sinking lines fall with a level attitude, because weight is added proportionally throughout the line to compensate for diameter changes. Scientific Anglers has such a product, which they call Uniform Sink. Level sinking lines do not have a "belly" between the tip and back taper, which hinders hook-setting and strike detection, and makes a fly ride much higher in the water than the line. Sink rate is labeled by "IPS" which means inches per second. Many are opaque in color. However, clear monofilament lines, originally called "slime lines," are hugely popular for clear water snooking in the surf, on the tidal flats or in clear water under lights at night. Unlike floating lines, full sinking lines must be retrieved nearly all the way in before the angler can make a pickup and re-cast.

Sink-tip lines are simply floating lines with a sinking tip section. Tip section lengths and sink rates vary according to a color code: The darker the tip, the faster the sink rate. A sink-tip line can be picked off the water to re-cast much like a full

floater, but many fly fishers complain about the fact that they are tricky to cast overall due to "hinging" at the junction of the floating and sinking sections.

Fly line out the tip-top, he's into the backing! Most anglers choose Micron or Dacron backing, but gelspun poly braid is gaining in popularity.

Leaders

Visibility is a factor with heavy monofilament, as is its effect on the action of smaller lures.

Your leader is where the rubber meets the road, and with snook you will need some traction. Due to the snook's affinity for structure, and its rough sandpaper-like lips and sharp gill plates, you must tie on a leader, unless your reel is spooled with 40-pound or heavier line, which would be an exception. Choose between monofilament and fluorocarbon. Snook anglers long used light to medium wire leaders and caught plenty of snook on live baits, plugs and jigs. That would work today, too, particularly at night or in muddy water, but anglers today are convinced that snook are too smart for that.

Before fluorocarbon hit the market, mono leaders were the snook angler's only choice. An angler concerned with stealth opted for about 18 inches of 15- to 20-pound mono leader to ward off the dreaded gill slice or structure tear. Most sensible snookers went a bit heavier, probably closer to 25- to 30-pound. But you should beef it up for bigger fish or night fishing. Forty-pound is fine, and there are times when 50-pound is better. Visibility is a factor with thicker mono, and the stiffness makes imparting action on most artificial lures much more difficult.

So, in the end, is fluorocarbon worth the expense? Many anglers think so. Fluorocarbon has less stretch, is harder to slice or fray, and is harder to see in the water than mono. The only time mono might take the place of fluorocarbon regularly is when fishing small poppers, because fluorocarbon sinks, and can alter the natural action of the smaller topwater lures.

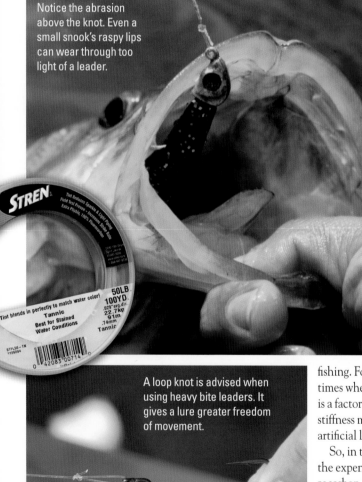

Notice the abrasion above the knot. Even a small snook's raspy lips can wear through too light of a leader.

A loop knot is advised when using heavy bite leaders. It gives a lure greater freedom of movement.

Leader Length:
Conventional tackle

With the basic understanding that a strong leader is essential for snook, the next logical question is, how long does it need to be? Fortunately, there are some easy to remember rules with this question.

Due to the abrasive nature of the teeth and the potential for gill plate cut-offs, any snook leader needs to be at least 18 inches regardless of the water conditions or relative tackle size. When fishing mono, this length might suffice. Just keep in mind that every hooked snook, landed or not, might require trimming some leader to bypass the fray so a little extra leader to start the day makes sense. More visible lines, such as braid, lead some snook anglers to lengthen their fluorocarbon leaders to 4 feet or so.

Fly leaders

Fly leader selections for snook are dictated by strata and personal goals. If you are hoping to stamp the record books, constructing an 8-foot leader that tapers from a 30-pound butt section to 20-pound to your desired class tippet,

followed by the obligatory 18 inches of shock will get the job done. Even if you could care less about breaking records, a tapered fly leader will help small docklight or flats flies roll over for a softer presentation. The overall diameter of

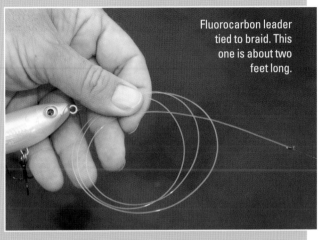

Fluorocarbon leader tied to braid. This one is about two feet long.

each section can be scaled down when targeting snook at dock lights or other areas where smaller snook are likely.

Snook fly rodders often opt for a straight section of leader, called the "homeboy" leader by some, and there are times when this simple approach makes perfect sense. When chucking large flies from a jetty, straight 50-pound test works. On the beach throwing poppers? Try straight 30-pound test. Working the dock lights at night can be done with 20- to 25-pound test fluorocarbon. Overall length should be a function of what length allows you to best turn your fly, as long as you stay within a range of 6 to 8 feet. SB

Choices in tapered leaders include commercial extruded leaders, left, and knotted leaders.

Hooks

ize and style of hooks for snook fishing are determined by the size of the bait, habitat fished and personal preference. On the small end, fly anglers might opt for a No. 6 or 4 J-hook for the flashy streamers used under the lights. Conversely, soaking a croaker under a bridge at night might call for a 5/0 or bigger circle hook. In open water, a thinner, wire-style hook might suffice. But when fishing in cover, a heavier hook will better stand up to the increased pressure needed to keep a fish out of structure. Most snook fishing is done in salt or brackish water, so hooks designed for saltwater applications should be used.

J-Hooks

J-hooks have been the standard for decades and are still a good choice in many situations. When livebaiting, wide-gap, shortshank hooks work well for snook. Long-shank hooks, which are ideal for fish with small mouths, are a poor choice. Regardless of what general style fits a particular need, remember that offset J-hooks tend to gut-hook fish more frequently than straight J-hooks.

Circle Hooks

The basic function of a circle hook is to find purchase in the corner of a fish's mouth. Anglers using live baits find they are extremely effective in preventing guthooking. All that is required is for the angler to avoid setting the hook in the tra-

ditional manner, which is easier said than done at first. With a circle hook, you simply allow the fish to eat, then reel up steadily to set the hook.

Jerkbait Hooks

A weedless soft-plastic jerkbait can be deadly on flats or mangrove creek snook. The hook is basically the same as bass anglers have been using effectively for decades. "Skinning" the hook, where the barb is brought back out just under the skin of the lure, strikes a balance between making the lure somewhat weedless and getting solid hookups. Many anglers call such a bait "Tex-posed," a play on the term Texas-rigged.

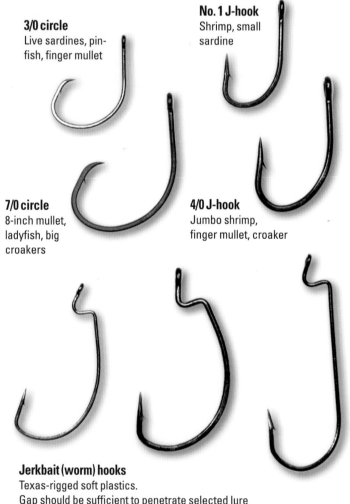

3/0 circle
Live sardines, pinfish, finger mullet

No. 1 J-hook
Shrimp, small sardine

7/0 circle
8-inch mullet, ladyfish, big croakers

4/0 J-hook
Jumbo shrimp, finger mullet, croaker

Jerkbait (worm) hooks
Texas-rigged soft plastics.
Gap should be sufficient to penetrate selected lure

Note: Hooks shown not in actual size.

Fly Hook Sizes

Here's an obvious statement to some, but worth a headline to most: There are hooks designed specifically for tying flies! Fly hooks are made of high quality steel, needle sharp, and designed so they will not chafe a leader. Depending on application, snook fly hooks generally run from No. 6 up to about a 3/0. The smaller fly hooks are perfect for working dock lights. On the other end, when targeting larger snook at the mouth of passes, a large streamer or bunker fly might require a sturdy 2/0 or 3/0. Within each size class, the strength, weight, and shaft length of the hook can be tailored to individual flies. A short, stout hook might be the perfect choice for a pudgy pinfish imitation, whereas a lighter, longer hook should get the nod for a Crease Fly or other popper. Ultimately, the size and style of the hook should be determined by the materials used, class of fly being tied, and the overall size of the fly.

If you are a beginning fly tyer, don't let these details keep you from bellying up to the vise. Ask your local fly shop owner what hook they recommend for a specific fly (don't forget to politely ask why). Once you have spent some time with their recommendations, you might note specific reasons to experiment away from the norm of hook style and materials, which might just lead you to the next "it" snook pattern. SB

There are hundreds of hooks designed for fly tying. Snook flies can be tied on anything from a tiny No. 6 to a 3/0 on average.

▶PRO TIP

Capt. Van Hubbard

Specialty: Live baiting

Location: Boca Grande, Florida

Rod: Spinning – 7 ½ foot, medium power, medium action

Reel: 2500-class spinning

Line: 10- to 15-pound poly braid

Leader: 20-pound or lighter fluorocarbon

Bait: Pilchard, Spanish sardine

Hook: Daiichi circle hook

Van Hubbard is a believer in circle hooks to prevent a snook from getting hooked deep. To prevent his live bait from fouling itself on the hook point, he places a plastic bead about ¼-inch from the barb. He typically hooks the bait through the nostrils. The "target bead" prevents the bait from riding up on the hook. When that happens with circle hooks, the point often gets buried in the backside of the bait. Van Hubbard prefers light leaders, even with live baits, to get more bites. When a circle hook finds purchase in the corner of a snook's mouth, the leader may not get frayed at all. SB

Angler lands a snook in a rubber-coated net. Small mesh is best because it lessens the chance that fins can be cut, which introduces disease.

Landing Gear

Rubber nets, bridge nets, slings and lip grippers give released snook a better chance to survive.

Snook are ornery characters next to the boat, and it helps to have a net or gripping device ready to subdue them. Gaffs are out of the question for a species which, in the U.S. anyway, is managed under tight slot limits,

Every precaution should be taken to ensure that snook you intend to release are not unduly harmed. Some biologists have indicated that holding up large snook by the lower jaw causes internal damage, leading to increased mortality. Using the correct handling and landing gear can help ensure the fish's survival.

The less time a fish spends out of the water the better, so many anglers release a snook without removing them from the water. With a good landing net or cradle, it can be much easier to control a snook in the water to remove hooks or take a quick measurement.

Some landing nets may cause more harm than good. The mesh size might be too large, the material too rough, knots too big, and hooks easily get caught in the netting material. Now it's easier to find nets with softer, smaller mesh that's even molded to eliminate knots altogether. Rubber-mesh nets are popular now, and lure hooks don't penetrate the rubber. For snook, consider buying an aluminum-frame net with strong enough mesh to handle the thrashing of a large fish.

Hoop Nets

Anglers on jetties, bridges, piers and spillways often fish several feet above the water. Removing a hooked snook from the water can be literally impossible without some kind of lifting device to get the fish from the water to the angler atop high structure. A hoop net is simply a deep net with a round opening, attached to long lead rope instead of a hard handle. A second angler is generally needed to lower the net to the water so that the angler with the rod can guide the fish into the net.

Snook in a small-mesh rubber net. Top, bridge (hoop) net and telescoping net.

Lip grippers help control fish boatside. But never hang fish by the jaw.

Gloves and Grippers

Consider wearing protective gloves when handling snook. A wet glove is much easier on the fish, as it is forgiving on the natural slime coating. But in the case of snook, the angler needs protection as well. The gill plates of a snook are serrated and sharp. A large thrashing snook can make a slice so fast the victim can see the results long before the pain sets in. To add further insult, the risk of infection due to bacteria in the water is increased exponentially when an open wound is introduced. And a snook's fin spines can make a nasty puncture.

A strong thumb hold on the lower lip is the best method of holding a snook. If it's a big one you plan to pull out of the water, get a second hand under the belly for support.

Lip grippers came on the scene with much fanfare. They allow you to grasp either the fish's upper or lower jaw and control it boatside. However, those with built-in scales made it standard practice among anglers to use the devices to lift fish out of the water without adequate midsection support. With mounting evidence that this may cause stress and even injury to a fish's internal organs and skeleton, it may be wise to simply use lip-grippers to hold fish still in the water while you remove the hook. If you want to take a quick snapshot, get in the habit of lifting the fish's head with the device and with a hand under its midsection. **SB**

Handle with Care

A fish-release sling allows you to lead a fish into it while in the water. Once folded around the fish (inset) the sling can be lifted and weighed with a lip-gripper scale. This model is designed by the West Palm Beach Fishing Club.

Angler has a snook under control and a net man in position.

Snook Fighting Fundamentals

Wouldn't it be nice if the only challenges associated with snook fishing were finding fish and then getting them to bite? Well, you still must bring your fish to hand. A snook is a crafty fighter that can get to structure in a blink of an eye. As they say, you have to get that fish coming your way, right now!

I remember standing on an ocean pier, looking down into clear water as a giant snook held in the current. A huge shrimp drifted toward the fish, and the snook slightly shifted to intercept it. The snook's head "expanded," the gills flared out, and the shrimp disappeared. In a flash, the snook returned to its original position like nothing happened. This sight reinforced my hook-setting strategy. If using a J-hook with bait, flies, or any lure, set the hook hard and fast. Turn that snook toward you as fast as you can by reeling as you strike, because when a big gal makes her initial dash for cover, any pause in your hookset gives

A snook is a crafty fighter that can get to structure in the blink of an eye.

the snook a chance to spit the lure or bait. Keep your rod in front of you; it does little good when it is has a severe "C" in it way overhead. An immediate hookset significantly reduces the possibility of gut-hooking a fish.

The key to successful hookups with a circle hook is to not set the hook at all. Rather, immediately point the rodtip down and away from the fish, and reel the line tight. Keep pressure on the fish, but never jerk to set the hook.

Occasionally a hooked snook that makes it to structure can be brought out, especially if you fish with braided line. The trick is to open the bail, if using spin gear. With casting gear, freespool with light thumb pressure. Then take the pressure off the fish and wait for it to swim free on its own. Then put the boots to the fish again. But more often than not, you'll have to maneuver your boat around pilings, or perhaps pass your rod between dock cross members or something similar. You may even consider bailing out of your boat (providing it's shallow enough and the bottom isn't deep mud) to get your fish unstuck. Such scenarios produce good stories to tell later, but few landed snook. SB

Snook Boats

There is a boat on the market for every style of snook fishing under the sun. On opposite ends, snook are caught from kayaks in the tiniest creeks and snook are caught from sportfishers in the biggest inlets. In between, options abound for every type of snook angler.

If you were forced to pick one boat to fish the multitude of snooky environs, it would be a small center console or larger bay boat. The ability to fish in waters less than two feet deep while still being able to fish passes and inlets covers most bases.

It is said that the boat doesn't make the angler, but a well-outfitted fishing machine, used in the right manner, will make your snook fishing more productive.

See DVD for more on choosing your snook boat.

A kayak gets you into skinny water quietly. A flats skiff, above, is suited for shallows, too, and increases your range.

Bay Boats

If you plan to fish a variety of habitats for snook, a bay boat is a solid choice. With an average length of 21 feet, a bay boat affords room for up to four anglers without giving up much in the way of stealth or draft. Wide gunnels allow for flush rod holders at many handy locations in the cockpit. Most have ample, or at least adjustable, fore and aft seating. Although most bay boats are big enough to provide comfort and relative safety, they are still small and light enough to be propelled with an electric trolling motor or motors, which many snook anglers consider essential. Tackle and dry storage space is typically ample for up to four anglers. Copious deck space houses baitwells, tackle hatches and more. More storage is possible if the rig has a big center console. Some owners add a T-top with an overhead box and rod holders.

Bay boats are commonly seen in inlets and passes, and they are ideal for backcountry rivers, creeks, bays and even the flats where the water is over a foot deep.

Nearly all in this class are V-hulls, defined as having some entry angle on centerline from transom to bow. But unlike vessels designed for offshore use, the typical bay boat has a shallow—or modified—vee, usually less than 19 degrees at the transom. Twin-hull power catamarans are also available in bayboat layouts.

Bay boats are light enough to be propelled with one bow-mount or two stern electric motors.

Bayboat anglers work a shallow shoreline. Left, a fine Florida bridge snook.

Many bay boats combine a flat bottom aft for shallow draft with a sharp entry to smooth out the ride on choppy days.

Left, bayboat center-console tackle drawers and rod racks. Right, one of multiple livewells.

Poling Skiffs

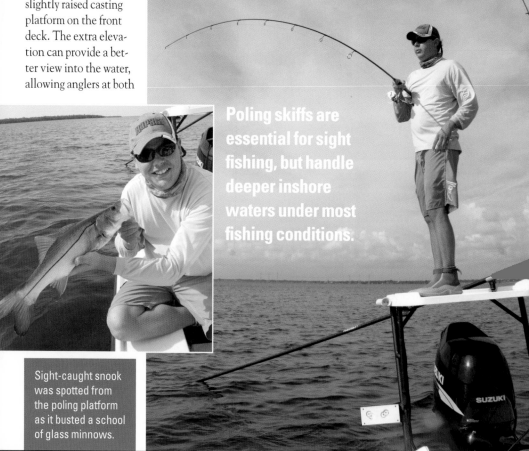

The flats skiff with a poling platform is not strictly reserved for bonefishing or tarpon fishing. It's ideal for much of snook country, too, even when sight fishing is not on the agenda. Today's flats skiffs range from 15 to 20 feet, and carry lots of gear, bait and safety equipment. Many have one or two livewells as a standard feature; plugged, these wells become additional tackle storage. Fly anglers have long appreciated flush-mounted cleats and deck hardware. When battling a monster snook in a tight estuarine river or spill-way, the freedom to step in virtually any direction without fear of tripping or slipping is valuable.

Many skiffs now dot the horizon with a poling platform aft and a slightly raised casting platform on the front deck. The extra elevation can provide a better view into the water, allowing anglers at both ends of the boat to see submerged points of interest from greater distances.

Not all skiffs deliver a bone-jarring ride on choppy waters. Experiments with the angle of bow flare, modified V-hulls and load placement have led to engineering marvels that can be surprisingly comfortable. With special attention to reducing hull slap, a modern skiff is a stealthy snook-hunting machine. Some classic backcountry skiffs, built decades ago, provide remarkable rides. The tradeoff is usually draft and noisy hull-slap at rest.

Poling skiffs are essential for sight fishing, but handle deeper inshore waters under most fishing conditions.

Sight-caught snook was spotted from the poling platform as it busted a school of glass minnows.

Flat-Bottom Boats,
Aluminum and Fiberglass

Some hardcore snook fishermen don't bother with the big-water bays; instead, they spend the year poking around canals and mangrove-lined backcountry creeks. For these guys, john-boats and flat-bottom fiberglass skiffs offer versatility and durability at a low price. A 14- to 18-foot skiff in this class can be powered with a 10- to 40-horsepower outboard, making for an affordable and fuel-efficient package. Many fishermen outfit these boats with bow-mount trolling motors for plug-casting shorelines. Some add a poling platform for accessing extreme shallows. Others forgo the extras and merely anchor in a likely hole and soak bait, a timeless approach that probably accounts for more snook catches than any other.

An aluminum john-boat converted for serious snook fishing.

Aluminum hulls are judged, and therefore priced, in terms of aluminum quality and thickness. All-welded models tend to last longer than riveted boats in salt water. Tunnel models permit some-what shallower on-plane operation, as the engine may be mounted higher on the transom. Which leads to a natural question:

Is an all-metal boat the best bet for traversing abrasive oyster bars and other hazards?

Intuitively it would seem so, but keep in mind that fiberglass is easier and less expensive to repair than aluminum, assuming you don't rip the bottom completely out of that glass boat. At the same time, small scratches and dings in aluminum don't require the constant maintenance that fiberglass gelcoat demands. As with any class of vessel,

buy the boat that fits your budget and angling style. Plan your adventures around prudent seamanship. There's no such thing as an indestructible boat. SB

Top, a skiff-bayboat hybrid. Bottom, a technical poling skiff for stealth in the skinniest of water.

Canoes

The traditional canoe can be a great snook-fishing vessel, especially for one angler and a partner. The typical inshore saltwater canoe is between 14 and 16 feet long, with a beam

An open-water canoe snook. This craft excels in the narrowest creeks where other boats can't go.

of at least 30 inches. There is ample space for tackle, safety gear and coolers. At a glance, most canoes appear to be essentially the same—pointy at both ends and somewhat flat on the bottom, usually with two bench seats for passengers. A closer inspection would reveal that canoes can be highly variable from one to the next. Some are designed for completely different purposes.

As you might expect, a narrower canoe will be easier to tip, making stand-up fishing difficult. The direct tradeoff is speed. A narrow hull will be faster than a wider one of the same length.

A canoe bottom that is completely flat might have been designed with a little whitewater paddling in mind. You aren't likely to encounter heavy rapids when snook fishing in Florida, but a flat-bottom canoe might last longer around oysters and other nasty structure in skinny water. However, a flat-bottom canoe is harder to steer and will be more affected by cross breezes. Some canoes have a crease that runs the centerline from bow to stern. Even a 1-inch lip can greatly improve the tracking characteristics of a canoe, reducing some of the side-to-side action when a single angler is paddling. The downside might be that a smaller hull area is faced with the brunt of the scratches, dings and poundings, resulting in a weak spot.

Kayaks Kayaks are superior

A kayak is a terrific mode of transport for the solo angler. With the lowest profile and weight of all boats, and silent, efficient paddle (or in some cases pedal) power, kayaks have grown in popularity among snook anglers.

Suitable snook kayaks run about 14 feet in length, with a beam of around 29 inches. Sit-on-top kayaks, easy to slide on and off while wade-fishing, are more convenient than the whitewater-style boats. Look for drain holes in the sitting area. Built-in rod holders are a plus.

One of the biggest advantages of kayaks over canoes is lower profile. Traveling across a wind can be a chore for a single angler in a canoe, but a kayak seems to slip under all but the stiffest winds. A drift sock can significantly reduce your drift speed when you are working a flat or pass, giving you multiple casts at each snooky looking ambush point. Affixing a trolley system to move your anchor from fore to aft allows complete control of which direction the boat faces in the current or wind.

If there is a downside to kayaks, it is storage space. Manufacturers have addressed this in different ways. Some kayaks have a space directly behind the angler that is the exact measurements of a standard milk crate, allowing the creative snooker to outfit the vessel in unique ways. Some models have oversize hatch covers, with storage that can hold an arsenal of rods.

The relationship between overall weight and durability goes a long way in determining how much you will spend on a new canoe. Canoes can be molded from materials such as Royalex or Kevlar, which is used in the military in bulletproof vests and helmets. In general, if you are looking at the newer materials that offer super durability and weigh less than 70 pounds, you can expect to pay more. Aluminum and fiberglass hulls last for decades, and just like that old Mitchell 300 reel that your buddy keeps scouring for in the pawn shops, some "paddle heads" will always stick with what has worked in years past.

The squareback canoe is a special vessel designed for propulsion under paddle stroke or outboard power. A portable outboard of 10 horsepower or so can be bolted onto the flat transom, taking some of the grunt work out of long trips. These vessels are usually wider and more stable than double-enders and may accommodate small poling platforms. SB

to canoes when it comes time to cross open water on windy days.

Top, kayak with rod racks, storage and staking pole. Below, GPS and VHF. Right, hull stabilizers permit stand-up fishing.

CHAPTER 5

Rigging a Snook Boat

What in the world would some old, crusty Florida snook fisherman in a leaky wooden rowboat have said 50 years ago about some of the fancy bells and whistles on snook fishing boats today?

Maybe, "Where were those toys when I needed them?"

Or, more likely, "Who couldn't catch a snook or two with all that help?"

It's your choice whether you want to be a minimalist, or dress out your rig with remote-control trolling motors, a hydraulic anchor, multiple livewells, chartplotters, bottom machines, side sonar, and poling and bow casting platforms to go snook fishing.

But there's little arguing that such additions can make fishing a bit more enjoyable. Custom rigging can make a not-so-perfect boat more suitable for a particular style of snook fishing.

Some add-ons are better left to factory rigging when a new boat is ordered. Others are relatively easy to install for the handier anglers among us.

A modern bayboat console with GPS, trim tab, jackplate and hydraulic anchor controls within reach.

Customize for Snook

Because snook are structure-oriented fish, trolling motors often perform double duty.

Fishing boats of all description are used to catch snook, but serious fishermen customize their rigs for special applications. Bare necessities for a general skiff or bay boat may include a durable trolling motor and a GPS for the deep backcountry, maybe a sonar fishfinder and a livewell for the inlet, and poling and bow casting platforms if sight fishing for snook is in your plans. Kayaks and canoes call for other specialized equipment.

Trolling Motors

A trolling motor can greatly enhance your fishing experience regardless of where you fish for snook. You'll enjoy enhanced stealth and close-quarters control that even the quietest 4-stroke outboard can't deliver. Electric motors are right at home on bay boats, skiffs, twin hulls, and even paddle craft.

Electrics provide maximum direction control and fast response when bow-mounted. This is a major consideration if your fishing involves tight maneuvering. Another option is stern-mounted single or twin motors, either on dedicated brackets or on trim tabs. Independent control of each motor gives an angler the ability to run motors in counter directions for a better turn response. Smaller electrics suited for paddle craft are generally mounted aft. If a canoe doesn't have a flat back designed for mounting an electric, anglers generally mount them directly to the side right behind the back bench, affording the best control. A handful of canoe models are now even manufactured with trolling motors in mind.

Because snook are such structure-oriented fish, trolling motors often perform double duty. A snook fishing trip sometimes includes jumping from spot to spot in close proximity, where firing up an outboard engine may spook fish. Since current is such a factor in snook fishing, a trolling motor is a great option for holding the boat stationary for short periods of time while an angler

Top, a flats snook stalked via push-pole. Bottom, wrist band electric motor remote control.

Angler uses an extension handle to steer her electric motor.

Electric motors work in shallow water, but not so shallow that the blade cavitates and spooks fish.

takes multiple shots at a dock light or point before moving on to the next target.

Unless you buy a boat that includes an electric motor or motors in the package, do not retrofit your boat with a trolling motor without ensuring your new motor is in the right power range (measured in thrust-pounds), and has proper shaft length. Too long of a shaft will bash the bottom or structure you are trying to fish; that noise means

goodbye snook. Too short, and you are broadcasting your presence with excessive surface noise.

Options for electric motor controls are many, from a "hands-on" tiller to foot pedals strategically placed around the boat, or even handheld remote controls. Be aware that many electric motors are designed with bass anglers in mind. A freshwater motor might not even last through a single (very short) snook season.

Left, poling platforms are a must for snook sight fishing. Right, pushpole can stake skiff in soft bottom.

Towers and Platforms

Height is added to fishing boats for one main reason: to increase range of vision. The increased viewing angle when standing atop a poling platform or casting tower, combined with a quality pair of polarized glasses, opens a window into the world of snook.

Anchors and Anchoring Devices

Boating anglers rarely chase down snook on the move. There are exceptions, such as summer beach snook that cruise the troughs in between spawns, but in general snook stay put. Fishing in-lets, spillways, bridges and other fixed structures usually requires holding the boat in a stationary position.

For deepwater snook spots, anchoring may be the only way to go. Choosing the appropriate anchor depends on your boat size and bottom makeup. Often the best snook spots are littered with boulders, rip-rap, natural reef structure, storm debris and similar snook attractors. A fluke-style Danforth anchor weighing less than 10 pounds serves most powerboat needs. For paddle

Left, anglers drop the hook to fish a jetty edge, presenting lures from upcurrent. Right, a Danforth anchor and chain long enough to protect anchor line from abrasion caused by rocks, sharp shell and other debris.

A bow casting platform affords a slightly better vantage point to spot cruising or laid-up snook.

Console towers gained popularity in the 1990s among Florida Gulf coast guides and anglers. The advantage of an additional 8 to 10 feet of height allowed anglers to run along a river channel or a flats edge while eyeballing surrounding mud flats for both snook and redfish. Of course, there is a point of diminishing returns—anglers in such high perches are also more visible to snook. But

the operative word with tower fishing is run, and running along a flat rather than fishing via pushpole is not every angler's cup of tea. In fact, running over the shallows becomes detrimental if done to excess. It puts wary snook on alert.

Conversely, a traditional aft poling platform gives you plenty of height to spot fish while poling along quietly. It also adds poling leverage and control that you can't enjoy from lower in the boat. There is no argument that killing your outboard and stalking silently gives you an edge. Snook tend to hold tight to potholes, oyster bars, debris and edges, where they feed as ambushers. From the poling platform you can spot a fish, or such structure, from quite a distance. Then it's just a matter of planning your approach for a cast.

craft, claw-style anchors that fold down to the size of a fist might be sufficient. Rubber-coated "one-piece" anchors, such as a mushroom anchor, hold smaller boats and can be super quiet.

In shallow water, a stakeout pole is handy. You push the end of the pole and tie off to either the stern or the bow. An automated, remote-control pole is even more convenient, though more expensive. Deployed from the transom, the Power-Pole somewhat resembles a giant mechanical scorpion stinger as it whips out and down into the bottom. Paddling anglers can employ a similar "staking" tool, such as a PVC pole, or the Stick-It Anchor Pin, a device that is jabbed into the bottom and lashed to the boat. SB

The Power-Pole stake-out device holds a boat over hard or soft bottom.

Bow casting platforms are typically a foot or so high, affording just a bit more height so that the "rod man" can see basically what the "pole man" is seeing. The slight increase in height can also add length to casts when needed. Some casting platforms even include a back rest for extra support.

Electronics

Need to find your way there and back? Navigate unfamiliar waters? Global Positioning Systems (GPS) are getting smaller, cheaper and incredibly detailed. For exploring new areas, marking your way in and out of mazes of mangroves, or saving coordinates of a sweet spot for a later date, the learning curve for anglers is cut way short. There is no substitute for studying maps (even online satellite maps such as Google: Earth). A paper backup is a good idea in case your GPS takes a swim. Leaving the dock without electronic mapping and positioning equipment (and at least a cell phone) no longer makes sense.

Fish-finding sonar is also valuable, due to the connection between bottom relief and snook. Since snook waters are often tannin-stained or murky, and many snookers fish under the stars,

visual contact of submerged relief is not always an option. When trolling a canal, finding the slightest ledge can mean finding a concentration of snook. Obviously, marking bait within the vicinity of known snook structure is a great sign.

Livewells

Live baits for snook can range from the tiniest of shrimp or minnows to foot-long mullet. The most dedicated snook anglers prefer two livewells. One should have enough water capacity and sufficient water exchange to hold mullet, croakers, pinfish, or large numbers of smaller whitebaits such as

Top left, compact GPS plotter for a small console. Above and below, recirculating baitwells.

scaled sardines or thread herring. Since it is illegal in Florida to possess a snook that is out of season or out of the slot limit, a release well is perfectly suited for such bait.

Baits are not created equally, so your baitwells might need some tweaking if you plan to transport

Know your Temp

A recent poll of snook anglers conducted by the Snook Foundation asked which piece of electronic equipment was a must-have. The answer surprised many—it was a water temperature gauge. Snook seldom feed when the water temp is below 70 degrees. A single degree can make a difference. Adjacent flats, or even sun-baked shorelines versus shady shorelines in winter, can be worlds apart in terms of fishing success. During the cooler months, find the warmest water and you are on your way to catching snook.

Depth	ft	Temp	°F	Speed
6.3		75.6		

different kinds of live bait. Here are a few general rules to consider: Use a square tank design when keeping non-schooling fish, such as pinfish, shrimp or crabs. Oval designs excel for schooling baits such as greenies or mullet. If your well is round and you are keeping shrimp, put something in the tank they can cling to. Leaving the dipnet in the well works, or drop a brick with a cloth tied to it. A bilge pump that moves 360 gallons per hour should suffice. Just remember, certain species of fish require higher oxygen levels, so don't overcrowd these fish unless you have an oversize pump. Use frozen water bottles to cool your well so you don't

introduce tapwater chemicals as the ice melts. An aerator placed at the bottom of the well that produces small bubbles keeps baits frisky.

Shrimp, crabs, or a half-dozen small baitfish can be kept in good shape in a bait bucket or small, portable livewell. Canoeists and kayakers can fabricate an adequate well from a 5-gallon bucket paired with a battery operated bubbler, or a more elaborate pump with a pickup. Shimano and Hobie now make kayak livewells that run on a compact 12-volt battery. To avoid deadly ammonia buildups, replace water frequently or install a small bilge pump. SB

Rod Storage

If you are determined to catch snook in every conceivable scenario, you'll need to acquire a variety of fishing tackle and become reasonably proficient with all of it. Chances are you'll find yourself doing everything from soaking baits to flinging flies in the course of a fishing day. Or, maybe you'll get in the habit of rigging a bundle of rods with different lures. Either way, you'll need serious rod storage in your boat.

Powerboats should have storage for 8 to 12 rods, including horizontal racks under gunnel and out of harm's way, and on the console, within easy reach. Aftermarket PVC holders can be mounted behind the helm, alongside the center console, or back near the outboard or poling platform.

Six rods or more might not be practical when fishing from paddle craft, but three or four is manageable. Canoes can be outfitted with rod holders, not to mention small coolers and milk crates. Most fishing kayaks have at least two flush rod mounts in the hull, and attachable mounts like the Scotty Mount can be placed anywhere on the hull. Remember to follow installation guidelines to keep the new mounts waterproof. SB

CHAPTER 6

Tides

The relationship between snook and tidal current cannot be overstated. Tides are the driving force behind everything a snook does throughout its life cycle. The transport of fertilized snook eggs from the passes and inlets to the safety of the salinity barrier deep within an estuary is a function of tides. An adult snook's ambush feeding style is dependent on tidal currents.

Opportunistic snook, like many gamefish, are relatively lazy and content to let their food come to them. In fact, every physical characteristic of a snook is tide-related—from its muscles and nervous system designed for quick, successful attack, to the oversize mouth that literally sucks up anything that the tide carries within its reach. If a snook was required to chase down its prey in open water, in the manner of tunas or mackerel, it wouldn't stand much of a chance. But within the tight confines of coastal waters, where tidal currents are squeezed and shaped by a variety of structures, the snook is an efficient predator.

If a snook was required to chase down its prey in open water, in the manner of tunas or mackerel, it wouldn't stand much of a chance.

Snook facing the
current, waiting for
prey to be swept
into reach. Above,
mangrove shore-
line at low tide.

A flood tide allowed this snook to access a mud flat where this angler spotted it before casting.

Tide Basics

Land masses and the often bizarre properties of wave energy affect the patterns of water movement as related to tides.

The moon, the closest heavenly body to Earth, has much greater gravitational pull and thus influence on tides than does the sun. As the moon orbits Earth, roughly every 28 days, the surface of the oceans nearest the moon is pulled away from Earth, creating a bulge. On the opposite side of Earth, water bulges in that direction as a result of centrifugal force.

The sun is the other major tidal influence. The relationship between the sun and moon, for the most part, is what gives us the tidal phases of neap and spring tides. A spring tide has nothing to do with the season of the year. In this case, "spring" comes from a Germanic translation of "jump," and indicates the highest tidal phases. This occurs when the sun and moon are pulling the Earth's water in the same direction, creating a synergistic effect where the combined effect is greater than the sum of the individual parts. New and full moon phases occur when the gravitational pull is coordinated in the same direction. Conversely, when the sun and moon are in conflict, their efforts somewhat counteract the tidal effects. We refer to this phase as a neap tide, which most effectively dampens tidal strength during "half-moon" (actually first and second quarter) phases.

Land masses and the often bizarre properties of wave energy affect the patterns of water movement as related to tides. If you were to examine snook fisheries in continental U.S. waters in three geographic regions—Florida Atlantic, Florida Gulf and Southern Texas Gulf—you would find three distinct tidal patterns.

Florida's Atlantic seaboard experiences a consistent semi-diurnal tidal phase. This means that there are two distinct high tides and two distinct low tides each and every day, with the slack transitions roughly six hours apart. In other words, if you fished a 6 a.m. high tide at the Lake Worth Pier in Palm Beach County, you can expect the next low tide to occur at about noon with another high slack tide coming just after 6 p.m. The moon orbits the Earth in 24 hours and roughly 50 minutes, so a semi-diurnal cycle occurs roughly 50 minutes later each day. Thus

Get to Know Your Tides

This graphic shows that neap tides, which occur when the sun and moon are not in line with Earth, are relatively weak. Spring tides, occurring during full and new moons, are stronger because the moon and sun are aligned with Earth, thus combining their gravitational pull.

Neap Tide

First quarter

Ocean level

Spring Tide

Low tide

New moon

High tide

Full moon

This extremly high Florida Gulf coast spring tide occurred during an autumn new moon.

the next morning's high tide should peak somewhere around 6:50 a.m., and so on throughout the month. A glance at the Miami tide chart in *Florida Sportsman* magazine or the *Florida Sportsman Fishing Planner* reveals a very consistent, two-peak sine curve throughout the month.

Across the Gulf in Texas, anglers experience only one high and one low each day. This is called a diurnal tidal pattern. You will observe a more noticeable shrinking of the peaks and valleys as the moon wanes from full toward the third-quarter moon. As it wanes further, to new (dark), the tidal variations will again increase, and the process repeats itself with perfect mathematical efficiency.

In Southwest Florida, the tidal pattern is influenced by the Atlantic Ocean, the

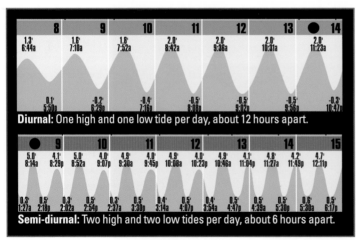

	8	9	10	11	12	13	● 14
	1.3' 6:44a	1.6' 7:10a	1.8' 7:52a	2.0' 8:42a	2.0' 9:36a	2.0' 10:31a	2.0' 11:23a
	0.1' 5:50p	-0.2' 6:29p	-0.4' 7:16p	-0.5' 8:08p	-0.5' 9:02p	-0.5' 9:56p	-0.3' 10:47p

Diurnal: One high and one low tide per day, about 12 hours apart.

	● 9	10	11	12	13	14	15
	5.0' 8:14a	4.1' 8:29p	5.0' 8:52a	4.0' 9:07p	4.9' 9:30a	4.0' 9:45p	4.9' 10:08a
		4.0' 10:23p	4.9' 10:46a	4.1' 11:04p	4.8' 11:27a	4.2' 11:49p	4.7' 12:11p
	0.3' 1:27a	0.5' 2:18p	0.3' 2:02a	0.5' 2:54p	0.3' 2:37a	0.5' 3:30p	0.4' 3:14a
		0.5' 4:07p	0.4' 3:54a	0.5' 4:47p	0.5' 4:39a	0.5' 5:30p	0.6' 5:30a
							0.5' 6:17p

Semi-diurnal: Two high and two low tides per day, about 6 hours apart.

Moving water is only half of the equation. Structure is a magnet for snook, and as water flows around it, the disruption of flow generally creates an area of reduced flow. The down-tide side of a dock piling, boulders at the bottom of a seawall, a pothole in the middle of a flat, or a mangrove island in the back of an estuary will have "pockets" of slower water that snook find ideal for ambush-feeding and resting. A snook can sit perfectly still and wait for shrimp, crabs or baitfish swept along by the current. With this in mind, the general rule of thumb when scoping a new snook spot is to consider the direction of water movement, and try to guess where the eddy would be. If you guess that a snook is looking into the tide from behind some form of structure, you will be right more often than not.

Some ambush spots are only productive during

Caribbean and the Gulf of Mexico, which creates a much more complex "mixed" pattern. On some days, St. Petersburg, Florida sees two distinct high tides (usually following a new and full moon). On other days, usually following the neap tides, the high and low tides merge to a resemble more of a diurnal tidal flow. Florida's lead snook biologist Ron Taylor once said that snook fishing in his neck of the woods, the Tampa Bay area, was best on days that had two distinct high tides.

Tides are measured vertically, as in distance above or below mean low water. Of course, this vertical movement creates a horizontal flow, or current. And as all snook anglers come to discover, a snook will feed more aggressively in moving water.

The high tide water line is apparent on this spoil island at low tide.

certain stages of the tide. Mangroves in estuarine headwaters (closer to fresh water) might produce best during a high tide. At the lower half of the tidal cycle, there might not be enough water to allow snook to feed, so they might move out to deeper water along with the prey. Fishing the potholes of deeper flats can work perfectly during a low tide, but that same spot during high tide might be relatively devoid of feeding snook.

Some might call snook lazy, but in truth they

have perfected an efficient hunting methodology. There are some points that are great ambush spots regardless of tidal phase, as long as there is some water moving through. An example of this might be the deep trough often found at either point of a mangrove island. A personal experience comes to mind, years ago when running past a protruding point of an island in Tampa Bay. My initial pass through was during a high ebb tide, and as I passed the point, I watched a dozen or so snook slide up over a submerged log which jutted into a very deep cut right at the foot of the mangroves. After several hours of fishing elsewhere, the tide was at low flood when I passed the other side of the island. This time, the snook were all on the other side of the log, presumably because the water was flowing in the opposite direction, which moved their prime ambush site to the other side of the structure.

Geographic Influences

Many landmasses and geographical features affect tidal currents in any given area. Local relief influences where and when water flows. Tides generally rush into deeper channels and bays first, and then push deeper into the back bays and shallow creeks. A large body of water immediately inside an inlet or pass receives a big tidal push. If the pass is narrow or shallow, the flow can be swift, creating hazardous boating conditions. In these extreme

Topography such as that of the Florida Keys, with so many flats and narrow bridge channels, makes tide predictions tricky.

conditions the best snook spots should be on the side of the pass that is receiving water, where snook can lie in the more gentle flow.

Permanent structure and land formations can change the times of tides that are reported for local landmarks, and if there was no other influence the changes would be very measurable. Unfortunately, there are other complications. For example, a huge storm far offshore can draw or push water in conflict with the predicted tidal heights. But the largest day-to-day tidal variable is wind. For example, after blowing consistently for three days, a nor'easter doesn't have to be all that strong to blow

all of the water out of a bay in Southwest Florida. This obviously creates concern for anglers fishing deep in the Everglades. On the other hand, these consistent blows can pack snook, tarpon, redfish and a host of other gamefish into very concentrated holes, which can create great fishing. In the absence of significant tidal flow, wind-generated water movement may produce tide-like currents, which can prompt snook feeding activity. SB

Above, strong winds may delay a tide change. Anglers fishing calm weather, below, timed the bite perfectly.

CHAPTER 7

Artificial Lures

Many long-time snook anglers, having fished their way through the livebait phase, prefer to catch their fish on artificial lures. It is more challenging to fool a big, wily linesider with a plug, jig or fly, and it enhances your sense of accomplishment. But you don't need any other reason to fish artificial lures for snook than that they work exceedingly well.

Sometimes, artificials out-fish natural baits because you can cover the water better with lures. You can get right to the fishing, rather than spending fishing time chasing live bait. Walking a top-water plug along a seawall; skipping a soft plastic under a dock; jigging a big bucktail at a spillway; gently dropping a streamer fly in front of a linesider on a flat—all are techniques that are dynamite on snook. The best part is that you can carry a basic selection of plugs, spoons, jigs, soft plastics, hooks and flies in one box to cover every snook-fishing scenario under the sun.

Live bait is deadly but it is far more challenging to fool a big, wily linesider with a plug, jig or fly. It enhances your sense of accomplishment.

See DVD for more tips on using artificial lures for snook.

Slim minnow-style plugs, top, can be deadly in clear water. Right, rattling suspending plug.

The Nature Fakers

A snook's high-set eyes tell you that it is an efficient surface feeder. Snook are not shy about crushing a topwater.

The main decision that anglers face when selecting artificial lures is whether to tie on something realistic that exactly matches the forage or some gaudy bait that triggers a reaction strike. When snook are feeding on big schools of baitfish, your lure that matches the bait may go ignored. Other times, it is the clincher. It pays to experiment by changing lures and presentations.

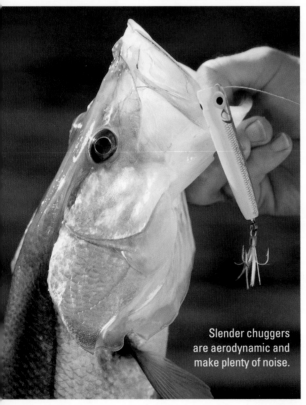

Slender chuggers are aerodynamic and make plenty of noise.

Topwater Plugs

Snook and topwater plugs go together like chicken wings and hot sauce.

One look at a snook's high-set eyes tells you that it is an efficient surface feeder. There are countless topwaters designed for saltwater use on the shelves

nowadays. But you can classify topwaters under a handful of basic subsets: chuggers, walkers, prop baits and floater-divers.

Chuggers (also referred to as popping plugs) have a cupped or hollowed-out face, and are among the easiest plugs to use. Twitching the lure creates a chugging or popping sound, replete with surface turbulence and bubbles that attract fish. You do not have to impart a lot of action—just use wrist action to twitch the rodtip during the retrieve. The harder the twitch, the bigger the splash. A chugger will effectively sound off and spit a good spray of water whether you work it continuously and rapidly, or pop it hard once between long pauses. These lures can be relatively blunt-nosed or deeply cupped, which affects the amount of sound and water displacement when the lure is popped.

They come in a variety of sizes and colors, with or without tail feathers, or trailing props. Some come with internal rattles. But rest assured, a chugger is loud enough without them. Most are one-piece, but some have a jointed body. Popular chugging plugs include the Storm Chug Bug, MirrOlure 87MR, Rapala Skitter Pop, and Tsunami Talkin' Popper.

Generally, snook like an active chugger, that is, something that sounds off but moves along the surface at a decent clip. Unless the snook tell you otherwise, that oft-mentioned bass style of plugging—pop it and forget it for awhile—usually does not work so well. That does not mean you should blast away maniacally either, especially in shallow water where such antics may spook a snook clear off a flat. You might try louder pops on a choppy surface or in dirty water, maybe tone down the sound on a slick surface.

The walking plug, the type with which the

Surface Talk

The classic walk-the-dog retrieve works best with so-called stick baits that have a cylindrical shape and sit high in the water. Here, an angler executes the retrieve with his rodtip close to the water which decreases the chance of slack forming in his line that can cause missed strikes. SB

popular walk-the-dog style of retrieve is employed, is normally cylindrical or shaped like a torpedo. This plug has no built-in action when cranked straight in along the surface. Walking the dog refers to that tantalizing side-to-side motion; it takes a bit of practice and the right rod action. When done correctly, the plug resembles a mullet or similar-shaped baitfish that is injured, and would like nothing more than to "leave the water."

Once the retrieve is mastered, a walking plug can be deadly, and especially on a relatively smooth surface. You basically retrieve the plug steadily and continuously at a moderate speed (eliminating all slack) while popping the rodtip with sharp flicks of the wrist. This makes the nose of the lure rise a bit while lunging alternately to the left and right. For first timers, a twitch every second or so is a good place to start. An experienced angler can control how far and fast the lure swings back and forth by timing the action. And there is no rule that says you can not pause briefly before resuming the cadence.

Topwaters include (top row) Rapala X-Rap Walk, Storm Chug Bug, Heddon Super Spook, MirrOlure She Dog, Sebile Ghost Walker. Bottom row, Bomber Badonk-A-Donk, Rapala Skitter Walk, Sebile Splasher, Rapala Skitter Pop.

The Heddon Zara Spook is among the original walking plugs, long favored among Florida snookers who ply mangrove cover, seawalls, the beach, bridges, and spillways where big snook hang out. But plenty of others are effective, such as Rapala's Skitter Walk, Sebile's Ghost Walker, Heddon's Super Spook and MirrOlure's Top Dog.

The length and width of a floater-diver's lip determines the depth it reaches when retrieved or trolled.

Floater-Divers

When retrieved, floater-divers look like baitfish struggling to get underway or heading for bottom cover. It gives you the best of both worlds—a wobbling bait on top, and if you steadily crank it, a subsurface swimmer. The degree of wobble and depth achieved depends on the length and width of its lip. Floater-divers normally look like slim minnows, and excel over shallow grassflats or oyster bars. With a combination of topwater action and wiggling, shallow dives, these plugs can present an irresistible target for most inshore gamefish. For snook, finding the ambush points and keeping the action close to likely spots is the best bet. Short retrieves, followed by a pause sufficient enough for the lure to float back to the top, imitates injured bait that makes an easy meal. You can drive snook crazy by twitching this plug repeatedly with rapid pops of the rodtip without moving it very far.

Under bridges and near docks at night, floating lipped plugs can be trolled across shadowlines in the upper two feet of the water column, or cast to pilings or along the edge of the shadows. With a slow, steady cranking speed, you can "wake" it along just under the surface, a deadly technique when snook shy from taking plugs on top. Trolling the plug might not be as exciting as seeing a big snook smash a topwater lure, but it can be a trip-saver. Examples of floater-divers include the Rebel Minnow, Cotton Cordell Red Fin, Rapala's Original and Jointed Series, Yo-Zuri Edge Minnow and Bomber Long A series.

Suspending Plugs

This type of plug is often called a twitchbait, and has slightly negative buoyancy. It should be

Rapala, Bagley, Storm, Corky and MirrOlure suspending plugs.

among your first choices for fishing subsurface around the shallowest structure, especially when you are not particularly concerned about covering a lot of water. Suspenders excel on snook that are reluctant to rise and smash a topwater plug. Stop retrieving and you can "soak" the thing in the strike zone for long periods of time. Ideal presentations include dropoffs, fallen timber in shallow water, potholes on shallow flats, and in the trough of the surf. Suspending plugs are popular with the night shift, too, and fish particularly well around lighted bridges.

Many look alike cosmetically and structurally, but there may be subtle differences in the way they fish. One bait may have a very tight wiggle when retrieved and hold a consistent depth. Another may have no built-in action whatsoever. Some have rattles, others don't. Some suspenders dive or rise slightly on the retrieve. Examples include the Sebile Stick Shadd, Yo-Zuri Crystal Minnow, Rapala Glidin' Rap and MirrOlure's MirrOdine series.

Sinking Plugs

Trolling oversize lipped sinking plugs along the deeper channels and river shorelines is a time-honored method. Snook anglers tend to go to sinkers in winter, or during the heat of the day during summer. A depthfinder is a huge asset when fishing this type of plug; it allows you to locate ledges, holes or other structure. The larger the lip relative to the lure body, the deeper it will swim. The packages of most are clearly labeled as to sink rate. Effective trolling plugs include the Rapala Magnum, Mann's Stretch series, Braid Viper and Storm ThunderStick series.

Hard-bodied lures with negative buoyancy might be the deadliest all-round choice for snook. Whether on the flats after the topwater bite has cooled, or dredging along pilings, piers, or even anchored ships, there is probably a sinking plug that fits the application.

Slower sinking lures, such as the 52M MirrOlure, have been standard snook catch-ers for years. Other choices include the Rapala Twitchin' Rap and CountDown, and MirrOlure's Catch 2000. Work these lures a little slower to get deep, but don't forget that some of them are

Left to right, Bagley, Rapala, Storm and Sebile sinking plugs rely on weight alone to run at various depths.

designed for the angler to provide some action via the rodtip. There are some plugs that sink very fast, such as the Yo-Zuri Edge Minnow, that can be fished deeper than 25 feet. Shipping channels or major passes (especially near the gigantic bridge pilings) are areas you might try. SB

Jig Styles

Despite the plethora of sexy plugs and soft plastics on the market, a jig is perhaps the most versatile snook lure of all. More big snook are caught on the bottom—why would you not fish a jig?

Jigs have no built-in action and are normally hopped along bottom when snook are the intended target. Jigs can be plain Jane or fancy and flashy. Most come in every color imaginable. But ask a veteran snooker which colors he uses, and you may hear white or yellow. You can fish a hair or plastic-tail jig pure, or tipped with fresh shrimp or a synthetic scent strip.

Jigs cast well for distance, and unlike some plugs and soft baits, are not as easily blown off course by the wind. They come in weights to sink to just about any depth, and can be dressed with natural and synthetic hairs of plastic and scented tails. Jigheads of all shapes are available, and are designed for specific applications. Common jighead shapes include bullet, boxing glove, Upperman (think lima bean), round, skimmer and more. Generally, the slimmer the shape, the faster the sink rate. The flatter or broader the head, the slower it will sink, given equal weight and jig dressing.

Where can you fish jigs? Under docks and bridges, in the surf, in the inlet, at spillways, in the backcountry—basically anywhere you find feeding snook, you usually have a chance to outsmart one with a jig.

Curly tail, paddletail and shadtail soft plastics can be matched to jigheads.

Practical snook jigs range from ⅛-ounce "bonefish" skimmers to the 3-ounce Flare Hawks, so popular with big-fish bridge anglers. But with the present snook slot limit, the Hawks have fallen off many snook anglers' radar screen. They simply catch too many 20-plus-pound trophies that can no longer go in the cooler!

In the shallowest water, skimmer-style jigheads are ideal because they ride hook-up, and

Assortment of bucktails tied on jigheads that ride hook-up are great for bottom fishing.

just as importantly, you can cast beyond a sighted snook and then hold your rod high and skim the lure along the surface to get it across the fish's path. Many have added mono weedguards for grassy bottom. Most popular weights are ¼ to ⅗ ounces.

Jig Dressings and Tails

Though many snook jiggers swear by bucktail for its breathing action in the water, anything from feathers to rubber legs can be used. Bucktail lends more buoyancy, so a slightly slower sink rate. Nylon material is more durable, yet lends little action. It can be somewhat translucent, like many

Shadtail with a skimmer jighead is ideal for fishing in shallow water.

baitfish. During the fall and spring mullet runs, large jigs like the Red Tail Hawk are standards at the beaches, inlets and passes. Possibly the best aspect of a jig is its versatility. Reeled steadily along the bottom, the lure can imitate a mullet or bunker foraging on the bottom.

Jigs were once dressed with hair, period. But in the late 1970s, plastic tails caught on with seatrout anglers. Eventually, snook anglers fell in line. Many plastic tails have built-in tail action. For example, curly tail and shadtail jigs undulate and vibrate whether you use a steady retrieve or employ the so-called "Florida whip," to make the jig rise and fall in the water. The size of the plastic-tail jig should be matched to local forage prey, and decisions for color choices should be based on water color and clarity. Jigheads with extra-long hooks accommodate longer jerkbaits. However, snook usually inhale the entire lure and tend to strike at the head anyway, so standard jighead hooks normally suffice.

Spoons for Snook

Before electric motors came of age in the salt, snook fishermen in the Everglades backcountry and elsewhere in Florida trolled along mangrove shorelines from point to point, with spoons wobbling in their wake. A Reflecto spoon with a yellow feather was the go-to lure. Spoons are still used, but most snook anglers turn to them for sight casting on

Single-hook spoons with weedguards for grassy flats.

shallow grassflats. Soft-plastic tails or feathers are commonly added to enhance the profile.

The most common error with spoons is retrieving too fast, causing the lure to spin. A slower retrieve will produce the desired wobble that entices snook on the flats. A spoon's width, shape and thickness determines its action, and depth can be controlled by slight changes in retrieval rate. A spoon can be skittered just under the surface by reeling with the rod overhead—a good technique for skinny water. Single-hook spoons are also great for side-arm skip casts under hanging mangrove branches or low docks.

In full sunshine and clear water on the flats, a shiny silver spoon might not work as well as a duller or darker shade. Many anglers prefer gold or even black spoons for snook. On the other hand, in cloudy or stained water, or during the twilight hours in the surf, silver is just the ticket. Add a plastic grub or curly tail to not only add appeal and action your spoon, but to soften the landing and decrease the chance of the spoon turning over and twisting the line. Also, consider adding a quality snap swivel to decrease line twist. Popular choices include the Johnson Silver Minnow, the Bagley Tri-Rattl'n Minnow spoon, Capt. Mike's Aqua Dream Spoon and the Nemire Red Ripper and Spoon Buzzer. SB

Soft Plastics

Snook on a paddle-style soft plastic. Below, Gulp! Jerk Shad and MirrOlure Soft Mullet.

Soft-plastic jerkbaits catch many inshore gamefish, so are not snook exclusive.

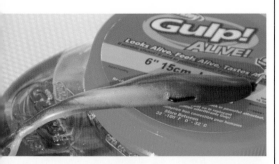

Borrowed form the bass-fishing world, soft plastics represent a relatively new genre of inshore saltwater lures. Most anglers call them jerkbaits, and they catch about every inshore saltwater species, so are by no means a snook exclusive. The variety of tail designs and body colors is complimented by different scents. As mentioned, some are designed to fish on a jighead. Others are fished Texas-rigged, mainly in shallow water or around hook-grabbing structure. Offset worm hooks are commonly used. Presently there are new keel-weighted jerkbait hooks, and those that have an independent, small screw attached that serve as a bait-holder and weedguard.

Skipping soft-plastic jerkbaits under mangrove branches or similar shoreline cover is quite effective. With the hook safely "skinned" back into the lure, you can cast much more aggressively without the fear of hanging up. If you do send your lure into the canopy, simply walk it out slowly, rather than jerking back.

The shape of the bait's tail will give you a clue as to how best work the lure. A straight, tapered, fluke-style tail is ideal when twitched just under the surface, while a paddle tail creates surface turbulence, a great effect on a choppy surface. Though nothing allows you to create the walk-the-dog surface retrieve like a topwater plug, an unweighted jerkbait with a straight tail does a credible job. By keeping your rodtip high, and imparting some rodtip action, you can make the soft bait zig-zag on top. And best yet, if a snook strikes short, you can simply stop and let the bait sink. Often, that fish will strike again.

Realistic Swimbaits and Plastic Shrimp

Stroll down the fishing dock at a snook spillway one rainy summer afternoon and you will likely see an angler casting a lifelike shad of some kind. Most are a weighted paddle tail shaped to look like menhaden, mullet, shad, freshwater panfish, pinfish and others. For the most part, these lures come ready to fish. The hook is already inserted and has a belly weight inserted.

D.O.A., Gulp! and Trigger X plastic shrimp models.

They are relatively inexpensive, which is good because your chances of salvaging the lure after a big snook has her way with it are slim at best. Makers of baitfish swimbaits include Storm, Tsunami, Berkley and D.O.A. Lures.

Plastic shrimp have been around for some time, though many anglers don't understand that they should be fished slowly for best results. Most are rigged on a single hook to swim headfirst, with a body weight to aid in casting. For the basic retrieve, let plastic shrimp sink nearly to bottom and then crawl it along, or manipulate it with sharp pops of the rodtip, and then allow the lure to sink again, and repeat. Plastic shrimp can be fished below a popping or rattle float as well. D.O.A. Lures packages a shrimp and float ready to fish, called the Deadly Combo.

Plastic shrimp are ideal for grassy flats, oyster bars, or under lighted docks and bridges. The next time you are fishing for snook around big baitfish schools, and you're baitfish lures fail you, fish a plastic shrimp under the schools. It can be a day-saver. Colors range from clear to dark brown. Manufacturers include D.O.A., Berkley Gulp!, Sea Bay, Storm and Trigger X. SB

Swimbaits are lifelike. Some have weight/hook inserts.

with a hook sticking up through its back. Why? They're easy to use, and they work.

This relatively new class of plastic jigs (swimbaits) have been enthusiastically embraced by snook anglers. Generally, these imitate baitfish

Snook Flies

Snook flies are either realistic "knockoffs" or attractors.

Snook are a terrific fish on fly tackle. Florida fly fishers in appreciable numbers discovered this over 40 years ago, and since then, have developed fly fisheries from the surf to the backcountry creeks of the interior.

Many snook flies are strictly attractors that suggest a life form, while others are truly realistic and designed to mimic the predominant bait that snook tend to target single-mindedly at times. Beaches adjacent to inlets and passes offer super opportunities, both for blind casting at dawn or dusk, or sight fishing when the light allows. And there is probably not a more effective way to pluck snook from under dock lights, mainly because fly fishers can present small streamers that mimic small baitfish in both size and shape.

Though many effective fly patterns are turned out by fly tyers expressly for snook, most saltwater baitfish streamers, shrimp patterns and poppers take snook. Everything from a tiny, 1-inch wisp of a minnow tied on a No. 6 hook to an 8-inch Deceiver tied on a 4/0 hook will take snook in a particular situation. Hard poppers made of balsa or foam, or deerhair-bodied divers appeal to surface-busting fish. They are dynamite for casting under mangrove shorelines and along seawalls.

Fly fisher shoots a minnow fly, below, to a dock light.

Everything from tiny baitfish streamers to big poppers take snook.

Watching snook that are stacked up under a dock light refuse lure after lure, and live baits, too, can frustrate the most patient angler. That's when a fly fisher in a skiff can ease up to a light, determine what the fish are feeding on, tie on a reasonable facsimile, and score again and again. It's largely a function of size. So-called docklight flies are shockingly simple and small. Imitating shrimp or little minnows that pass under the light on the tide, a fast moving wad of flash tied to a hook is usually just too much for a snook to resist. Neutral buoyancy eyes and some kind of flash tied into the body can enhance the fly. The key to this fishery is presentation. Experienced night fly anglers usually start working the fringes of the light, along the shadows, and work their way in toward the bright center directly under a light. Short strips are most effective, but at times a "dead drift" is the way to go. If there are no takers after the first few casts, switching to a slightly different variation of flies might be worthwhile. When you approach a very slow or slack tide, try throwing a small bass popper directly under the light. Work it as if you were fishing bass: pop, wait, pop, wait, and hold on!

There is an ideal fly pattern for every snook habitat and specifc feeding situation under the sun. Or, the moon.

Another scenario where tiny flies dominate is along the brackish and freshwater canals where snook congregate during the winter months. As they feed on tiny mosquitofish (gambusia minnows) a small streamer such as a Marabou Muddler Minnow, Glass Minnow or Conner's Glades Minnow tied on a No. 6 or 4 hook is the best bet.

Otherwise, daytime snook fishing calls for bigger flies. Streamers and sinking flies have proven to be very effective snook catchers. Along the mangroves, Deceivers, Bendbacks, Sea-Ducers, Dahlberg Divers and a wide array of mullet and pilchard patterns get the nod. White bodies work well in clear water; chartreuse and tan combina-

tions might be better in cloudy or stained water. In the surf, many fly fishers turn to more translucent baitfish patterns tied with synthetic winging materials. Clouser Minnows are always good, and fish well in most places a snook calls home. It is a great prospecting fly for flats potholes, shallow dropoffs and around docks, bridges, or in the surf. Wherever you fly fish, match the local forage to greatly improve your chances of hooking up. And always consider the rod you are casting. A fly is only a good choice if you can get it to the fish. Choose a rod and line that can handle the fly's size and weight. That way, fly casting remains fun rather than tiring . SB

CHAPTER 8

Natural Baits

I f you want to catch a big snook, or your first snook, and you're not particularly experienced with artificial lures, consider using a live bait. Live baits, whether baitfish or shrimp, can be the clincher with otherwise finicky snook. This is not to say live bait will ensure a successful trip. You still have to fish where the snook are. Season, habitat, tide, wind direction and strength, and time of day all have bearing on which live bait is best. Taking the time to observe which forage is predominant where you fish is half the battle. Then it's a matter of presenting your bait in a natural manner.

Live bait is only as effective as your presentation. Good livebait anglers catch the hardiest bait, keep it that way, and use proper terminal tackle to fish it.

See DVD for more tips on using natural bait for snook.

Top, pilchards shared by snook and heron. Right, yellowfin mojarra , pinfish and scaled sardine (pilchard).

Shrimp

Snook feed on shrimp throughout their life cycle. Whether you're after schoolie snook popping tiny shrimp under a dock light or big, overslot females blasting hand-size monsters riding a rushing inlet tide, shrimp are a dynamite bait. Winter and late-spring shrimp runs draw snook of all sizes to the inlets. But shrimp are available and effective in many situations throughout the year.

Shrimp are readily available, appeal to snook throughout the fishery, and can be rigged in myriad ways.

Just about every coastal bait shop carries live shrimp, though late summer sees dry spells, or shrimp that are too small for practical use. Show up early and ask for jumbos or selects. Those hand-picked shrimp go fast during open snook season. The bigger shrimp are hardier, easier to cast, and tend to swim better when freelined or presented under a float.

Caring for these baits is relatively easy. In an aerated livewell, they stay frisky with little fuss. Don't crowd more than a couple dozen into a single bucket, and keep 'em cool during the summer. If using a perforated, floating bait bucket, keep it in the water while fishing. Aerator tablets can help get you from point A to point B, but try not to rely on them for very long. If you lack a livewell or bait bucket, or want to buy your bait the night before a morning trip, use this trick: Place your live shrimp between layers of moist paper towels or newspaper, and place that on ice. Just keep the melting ice from reaching the shrimp, and they will live for hours.

Live shrimp fish best on light-wire hooks. Opt for the smallest hook practicable—a No. 2 or 1 hook should get the job done with most shrimp up to three inches long; larger shrimp require bigger hooks. Snook call for a bite (shock) leader. But with live shrimp, to keep them frisky, opt for the lightest test and the shortest length that you can risk to decrease drag in the water.

There are numerous hook positions for shrimp. If you plan to freeline live shrimp, insert your hook through the depression that runs just under the pointy horn (that sword that pokes you when you reach into the bait bucket). This hook position keeps shrimp alive for quite a while. Be careful not to pierce the dark spot (the brain). A sharp hook with a crimped barb will do even less damage to the bait and allow you to unhook a snook quickly.

To fish a shrimp deeper along underwater structure, and allow for natural movement, hook the shrimp in the same manner, then add some weight about two feet up the leader. A pencil lead or a few small split shots will do the trick. Remember that shrimp rarely swim against the current, so toss a shrimp upcurrent whenever possible so the bait travels downcurrent toward a dock, bridge shadowline, or similar snook haunt. Control your depth by raising or lowering

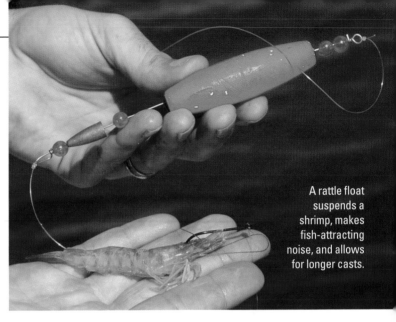

A rattle float suspends a shrimp, makes fish-attracting noise, and allows for longer casts.

the rodtip, and keep the line tight. Just because you have live bait is no excuse to become lazy. You can also freeline a shrimp after hooking it in the last tail segment. This works well when you want to fish tight to mangroves and keep the shrimp from the root tangle until a snook takes it.

Popping corks can come in very handy when fishing with shrimp. Use of a cork allows you to cast a shrimp much farther. Also, a pop or two tells a snook that another fish is feeding nearby, and investigation is warranted. On the flats, adjusting the distance between the float and shrimp allows the bait to drift above the grass. Allow the current to carry cork and shrimp over potholes, ledges or other structure. Of course, the cork signals a strike, too, which helps inexperienced anglers hook up.

For casting and retrieving fresh-dead shrimp, many anglers choose a long-shank hook. As you retrieve line, the shrimp appears to be retreating from a threat. Tear the tip of the tail off first, thread the bait until it lays straight, and bring the point back out on the underside. If the bait is not threaded straight, it will spin on the retrieve or when held in the current. That's a poor presentation, and it will cause line twist.

Perhaps the deadliest presentation of all is pairing a live shrimp with a bare jighead. The Troll Rite is a teardrop-shape leadhead poured on a strong hook, and normally painted white or yellow. It has a line-tying eye on the gap-side of the lure, so it rides hook-up, and can be vertically jigged. To attach the shrimp, simply pass the hook through the horn, from side to side, or from the underside (the chin) through the top of the head. This rig can be cast and retrieved steadily, or bumped along bottom, where snook do much of their feeding.

Above, jig-and-shrimp tandem is ideal for bumping bottom. Below, snip tail fin and thread shrimp on bare jig to make shrimp appear to retreat.

Baitfish

Mullet

The fall mullet run is responsible for more "sick days" among Florida fishermen than an entire flu season. The "mullet rain" caused by big snook or other predators attacking from beneath a hapless school of finger-size mullet is a wonderful sight for snook anglers along the beaches, at the inlets, and inside the Intracoastal Waterway. This fall feeding

Live mullet nose-hooked with circle hook for freelining subsurface. Top, a fresh mullet head rigged with a circle hook is deadly for big snook feeding on botttom.

frenzy can last up to a month.

Snook will charge through a wad of mullet and single out a "weak link," the one that can't keep up with its schoolmates. Best bet is to fish the fringes of the main schools. Work the top of the water column by hooking the mullet through the lips or anal fin. To present the bait on bottom, either hook it through the throat or dorsal fin, or hook it through both lips, from bottom to top, with a bare jighead.

Mullet are usually castnetted to get a quantity quickly, but are not particularly hardy when kept in an overcrowded livewell or bait bucket. They are relatively sturdy on the hook, however, so don't keep too many at once.

Large mullet, sometimes over a foot long, are prized by snook anglers who prowl bridges and spillways at night with heavy tackle, hoping to land and release a 40-plus-pounder. Snook are scavengers and big specimens will take a lip-hooked mullet head, or a mullet "plug," which is a beheaded mullet, soaking on bottom. This technique works well in passes and inlets, around jetties and in the surf.

Croakers

The Atlantic croaker is a smallish member of the drum family. They are relished by snook at the inlets during the spawn. In fact, croakers are so effective at catching snook in Florida, and south Texas, too, for that matter, the occasional discussion pops up about outlawing their use. When croakers are schooled, they are relatively easy to catch with a castnet. However, most anglers fish small hooks and chunks of shrimp to catch one baitfish at a time. It's a great way to spend some quality time with a budding young angler, but if you are more interested in getting after the snook rather than catching croakers, plan to hit the bait shops early. When in stock, croakers go fast.

Small croakers aren't especially active on the hook, so when fishing in shallow water you might consider fishing them under a float to keep them swimming above bottom. Hook a croaker through the back or near the dorsal fin. In the surf, switch to an egg sinker to keep the bait at the bottom, particularly when there is a swell. When fishing in light current, hook the bait in the tail. In ripping current, hook the bait through the nose or through both lips so that it faces the flow. Croaker, as the name implies, croak loudly. That makes them a good bait choice for dirty water or nighttime fishing.

Pinfish are an easy-to-catch baitfish over grassflats. Dorsal hook position is good for vertical fishing under bridges.

Pinfish

Pinfish are generally fished under a cork in shallow water. Always be mindful of current direction before casting out a live bait. Ideally, your bait should drift on the tide over a pothole or other potential ambush point. Hook your bait in the back just forward of the dorsal fin and peg the cork so that the bait swims just above the grass. It will struggle to swim down into cover, and this sends out sounds of distress that attract snook and other gamefish.

You can chum them into castnetting range or catch them one at a time on small bits of shrimp with small hooks. Check over the grassflats or at channel edges of the flats. This baitfish has pin-sharp fin rays, and snook typically swallow it head first. Large pinfish are strong swimmers that require substantial weight to keep them where you want them. If you are soaking big pinfish off a bridge or pier, heavy tackle is a wise choice because any snook that takes interest is likely to be a bruiser. Pinfish are hardy in the livewell or an aerated bait bucket so long as you don't crowd them.

❯PRO TIP

Capt. Butch Constable
Specialty: Mullet run in inlet and surf
Location: Jupiter, Florida
Rod: 7-foot heavy spin with fast taper
Reel: Penn 5600 SS
Line: 50-pound poly braid
Leader: 80-pound fluorocarbon
Bait: Live mullet
Hook: 6/0 or 7/0 J-hook

Constable has logged some 20,000 snook in his book, many of them 20 pounds or more, caught during the fall bait run in the vicinity of Jupiter Inlet. Constable prefers heavy gear to get the fish in as quickly as possible and release it in good shape.

"There is a lot of angler traffic during the mullet run," says Constable, "so you need to keep your fish away from other anglers' fishing lines."

Constable stresses that big snook are reluctant to leave the bottom to pursue their prey, so he perfected the "Jupiter Rig" to prevent a sinker from moving too close to, or far from, his bait. He ties a swivel to his braided fishing line, ties in a 2-foot piece of heavy monofilament, threads on an egg sinker, and then ties on a second swivel to which he attaches his 3- to 4-foot 80-pound bite leader.

Pilchards and thread-fin herring (top), a.k.a. whitebait, require roomy, well-aerated livewells.

Red eyes and noses mean stressed baits. Crowded livewells can cause this.

Herring/Menhaden

Atlantic herring, menhaden, scaled sardines and Spanish sardines are snook candy. These highly desirable whitebaits are common throughout the southern half of Florida during the spring, summer and fall. Snook follow the migrations of these baits like bloodhounds. They can be easily chummed into castnet range using bread or an oily, canned fish. A livewell filled with these shimmering, silver-white baits is as close to a sure thing as there is in attracting a snook to the hook.

These baitfish are extremely delicate when kept in the livewell, and require a large well with rounded corners and a good flow of clean water.

Freshwater Baits

Snook are familiar with freshwater prey, and spillway fishermen know that snook rarely turn down a plump shiner that is swept through water management structures after a heavy rain.

Just about anything that swims on the freshwater side will attract a bite; just keep the local laws in mind. It is illegal to possess a gamefish (such as a bass) that is under the legal size limit, regardless of whether you intend to eat it or feed it to a snook.

Further, a host of invasive tropical fish are fantastic snook attractors. Mayan cichlids (in photo at left) frequently get swept to the saltwater side of spillways, and are eaten by snook. In Florida, it's illegal to transport a living invasive fish, such as a cichlid or oscar. To stay safe, stick with the native freshwater forage fish. SB

Skimp on any of these details and your bait won't last long. Once hooked, they should be checked frequently to make sure they're lively. Their soft bodies dictate that anglers use slow-action fishing rods, which helps lob the bait long distances without ripping the hook from the flesh. The little dent right in front of a Spanish sardine's eyes is the perfect place to thread a small hook (1/0 is an ideal size), but larger baits can be hooked in the dorsal or at the tail as well. The smaller baits are best fished with very light tackle and line, with long spinning rods to achieve maximum distance when casting.

Popping corks can be added to control bait drift and add casting distance. Freeline these baits along the mangroves, at island points, or over depressions and ledges on the flats, and stay on the your toes. When a snook starts to zero in, these baitfish tend to panic at the surface just before a snook strikes. The larger whitebaits can be pinned to the bottom with a sinker or a jighead when fished at passes, inlets, piers and bridges. Even a dead herring drifted along the bottom will garner the attention of all sorts of predators, including some monster-size snook.

These baitfish are an important link in the ecosystem. They not only provide much needed protein to hordes of predatory fish and birds, but they are proficient filter feeders. The common practice of netting several hundred small herring and using them to chum snook into a feeding frenzy is viewed by many anglers as wasteful. Further, heavy live-chumming sounds a dinner bell for sharks and porpoise, who love to linger under boats and pick off tired snook as soon as they are released. An angler simply must make a decision whether to live chum after considering possible consequences. SB

Tiny Live Baits

Big snook will feed on surprisingly minuscule baits. During the cooler months, many snook move to the headwaters of rivers approaching the freshwater line. Once there, they feed on a few staples from their juvenile days—gambusia minnows, or mosquito minnows. These baits average about an inch long, but snook of all sizes will eat them. Birds of prey wading the shoreline can be a good indicator of both minnows and snook. On the flats, when

Schoolie snook launch an attack on glass minnows along a barrier island beach.

you see huge wads of glass minnows, you can safely assume that snook are lurking around the fringes of the bigger schools, waiting for the right moment to rush these protein-packed fish.

Unfortunately, it's tough to cast a tiny baitfish lure with a baitcasting, or even a medium-size spinning outfit. Fly casters do have the advantage in this situation because small glass minnow flies can be deadly. Stepping up the size just a bit, Florida Gulf anglers are wise to net a few chub minnows or killifish. They can run up to 3 inches long, and can be rigged on a hook. This baitfish is usually in the shallow waters, rooting around grass and macro algae, and are fairly common on the Florida Gulf coast. Drift-fished under a float, it struggles to reach the bottom, which catches the attention of snook. SB

CHAPTER 9

Snook Recon

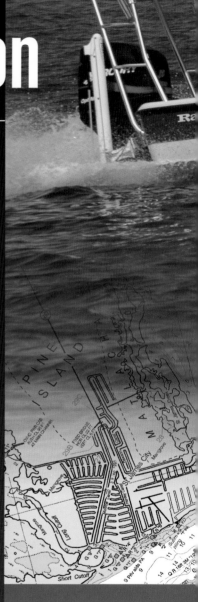

If you only refer to a nautical chart to navigate from point A to point B, you're not getting enough out of it. A chart also gives you a look at what's underwater. It can help you find the dropoffs, the hard bottom and grass, the submerged bars, spoil islands and depressions, and other natural relief—those structures that attract snook. Check out your chart's key and you'll quickly learn what every symbol means for the topography. You might be on strange waters yet quickly determine which spots hold promise for snook even before you launch your boat.

You could get along with a paper chart just fine. However, to keep up with technology, gaze at an electronic, or 3-D picture of the waters you are fishing. Global Positioning System (GPS) chartplotters that have fish-finding sonar functions give you a decided edge. But the best information is useless if you don't understand what to do with it. Take the time to learn how underwater topography and structure relate to current and a snook's feeding patterns, and you will extract the most knowledge from your paper chart or plotter. Some GPS chartplotters offer software for inland regions to help you explore the most remote snook waters in Florida.

GPS chartplotters that have fish-finding sonar functions give you a decided edge. Just the same, learn to recognize features with your own trusty eyes.

See DVD for more tips on finding elusive snook.

Even shore-bound anglers can spot good snook topography by learning what a chart key's symbols mean.

Zero in on Snook

Snook fishing can involve some deep exploration, and a GPS chartplotter gives you a "bread crumb" trail to get back home.

Many anglers purchase charts and electronics solely for the purpose of safety, and that's a good reason. No one wants to get lost or run aground—or worse—during a day's fishing. Hunting snook can lead to some backwater exploration, and a chartplotter or GPS gives you an electronic "bread crumb" trail to lead you back to your starting point. Handheld GPS units are affordable and sufficient as a main plotter and certainly good for a backup should your main electronics fail. However, the chance of electronic failure is very real. That's why you should carry a paper chart and compass for backup. With a little practice, this "old-school" combination will help you find your position by using cross bearings (getting compass bearings on two objects and then finding the intersection point on a chart to determine your position), or by dead reckoning

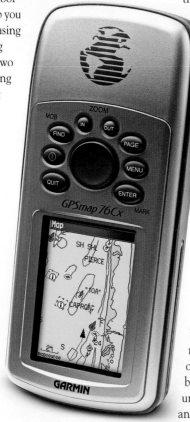

Handheld GPS chartplotters are affordable and portable. (But don't try to sneak one aboard your guide's boat!)

(where you determine your present position by projecting prior course steered and speed over the ground from a last known position). Exhaustive studies have proved that paper charts, compasses, and handheld GPS units are much more effective when taken out of the truck glove box and actually placed on the boat.

Charts

A quality navigational chart is superior to many of the "fishing spot" charts on the market, although fishing charts often have those big, bold abbreviations for fish marked hopefully, at all of the right places. A good navigation chart is more detailed in regards to contour lines, depth notations, and especially important to snook fishermen, structure symbols. Detailed explanations of underwater topography symbols can be found on NOAA Chart No. 1, which is not a chart at all, but rather a chart information guide with a key explaining all chart symbols. Color-coded contours tell you what is land (yellow shade), tidal flats (greenish yellow), and a shoal area (blue).

Any good snook fisherman knows that in a stretch of relatively featureless water, an oyster bar, ledge, dropoff, submerged spoil, rocky patch or channel edge can be golden. So take the time to get familiar with the symbol key and you'll cut out a lot of blind fishing. And then relate that relief to current. Tidal flow puts snook on the feed, but not just anywhere. To be considered prime snook territory, an underwater feature should provide refuge and an ambush opportunity.

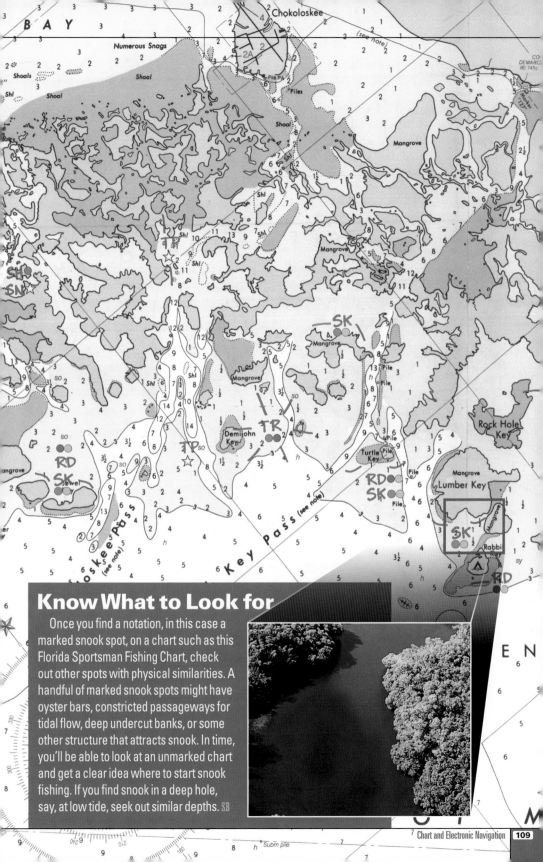

Know What to Look for

Once you find a notation, in this case a marked snook spot, on a chart such as this Florida Sportsman Fishing Chart, check out other spots with physical similarities. A handful of marked snook spots might have oyster bars, constricted passageways for tidal flow, deep undercut banks, or some other structure that attracts snook. In time, you'll be able to look at an unmarked chart and get a clear idea where to start snook fishing. If you find snook in a deep hole, say, at low tide, seek out similar depths. SB

Electronics

Great strides have been made in digital mapping in a short time. With a unit as small as your palm, you can scroll through detailed maps with details to the square meter. Plotting your location and travels through unknown waters has never been easier. Most base GPS or chartplotter units come with upgrade options, usually in the form of a memory chip, that take the functions to a new level. Some are specific to fishing needs, and include fantastic structural and topographic details. Tide and temperature can be calculated for you in real time. Learn how to tune your sonar and you can usually determine water temperature at various depths—a great piece of information to pinpoint a snook's comfort zone.

The man overboard (MOB) feature on every GPS can be your best friend, allowing you to mark your location when you locate a good snook spot. MOB tags are usually denoted only with a number, and "trigger happy" anglers might mark up to 50 in a day. Immediately coordinating this feature with a detailed log book that notes the structure and its value to you keeps your MOB marks from becoming useless numbers cluttering your view screen.

Handheld models today have many features of the bigger, mounted units, and they make sense for snook anglers who fish from kayaks, canoes, or simply prefer not to mount electronics on a small console. Most companies make a "water-resistant"

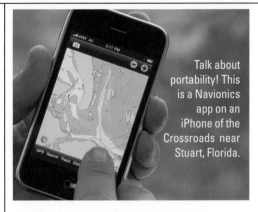

Talk about portability! This is a Navionics app on an iPhone of the Crossroads near Stuart, Florida.

model—obviously worth any extra cost.

Other helpful features common to most plotters include tide stage indicators, surface temperature gauges, and color screens that are easy to read in bright sunlight. Most units fall in the $400 to $1,200 range, with handhelds going for even less. SB

This bridge and its pilings are recorded in detail with side sonar on the screen of Humminbird's 1197c.

A NASA satellite image of Florida. Subsequent zooms in on Pine Island Sound provide more detail, below.

Tampa

Atlantic Ocean

FLORIDA

Gulf of Mexico

Ft. Pierce

Pine Island Sound

Ft. Lauderdale

Satellite Photos Lead to the Spots

You can get a preview of an area you plan to fish right from the comfort of home. Online sites such as Google Earth (www.earth.google.com) and TerraServer (www.terraserver.com) have amazingly detailed satellite images of the world, and that includes those snook-rich waters. You will gain a whole new perspective on fishing holes you thought you knew intimately, and it will give you a jump-start in getting a lay of the land in new areas.

Compare the images to your nautical chart and you'll see those submerged snook spots and depth contours depicted by symbols on the chart. Many anglers print out the sat images and use them in conjunction with their plotters and charts. There is a great tool now available, Fugawi's Google Earth plug-in for Marine ENC version 4.6. Simply connect to the Internet, select your fishing region and software will pull up and save corresponding Google images. You can now view imagery on location next to your chart while you are fishing or underway. With a GPS connection, the program works on PCs and PDAs. SB

Pine Island Sound

Satellite view of oyster shoals and the angler view of same, left.

CHAPTER 10

Snook Tactics

Snook bites tend to be short and sweet. They bite like crazy, then someone hits the switch off. What the snook bit yesterday may not get a sniff today. Snook can be fickle, and especially challenging, when the water is chockablock with forage. But snook are fish, and all fish must eat, so it's just a matter of being on the water when and where they are feeding. They are creatures of habit, so keep good records—of good and bad days—in a detailed fishing log, and you'll discover the patterns that help you catch more snook. Go about fishing haphazardly, like many anglers, and you'll just get "snookered."

Snook are widely distributed across the inshore waterscape, so the best snook fishermen make it a special point to master a wide array of skills and tactics.

See DVD for more snook tactics.

A mangrove point beckons and calls for pinpoint casting. Above, snook from a backcountry creek.

Pick Your Poison

If you're not plucking hardware from the branches once in a while, you're not snook fishing.

Angler casting a plug to mangrove prop roots, the classic snook lair.

G ood snook fishermen develop specific skills and use fishing tactics best suited for unique snook habitats. Though basic skills can be applied across the board, a polished caster will likely out-fish a live-baiter on the sight-fishing flats or when fishing pockets under mangrove overhangs in backcountry creeks. The good live-baiter, however, often clobbers the light-tackle caster at the jetty or the inlet. But no matter your approach,

This snook nailed a jig hopped over bottom at a creekmouth during falling tide.

once you get that strike and the battle is joined, you'll need to fight a snook efficiently, especially if you plan to release it to fight another day.

To emphasize how important casting accuracy is to snook fishing, picture this: Two inexperienced anglers are on a snook trip. At the first spot, they both cast toward a fishy looking point on a mangrove-lined shore. One angler gets hung up in the lower branches, the other casts 15 feet short of the shoreline. Which angler is more likely to hook a snook?

If you said neither, then you are right. But the short-caster just might luck out. At least his lure hit the water. But in this shoreline situation, a snook rarely swims 15 feet from ideal ambush cover to chase a piece of plastic. Not when it is used to its meals drifting on the current right past its nose. Plucking hardware from branches or other structure is part of the game. As they say, if you're not catching branches once in a while, you're not snook fishing. Same goes

for hanging a dock piling from time to time, though leaving a bunch of busted-off leaders on someone's private dock, docked boat or dock lines is disrespectful. If done at night, touching someone's dock to salvage lures might shut down a hot dock light for good. So cast aggressively, but accurately.

Learn a variety of casting strokes with different kinds of rods. For example, in the mangrove creeks, rivers and bays, snook may be most accessible on the bottom half of the tide. To show the goods to a snook, you'll often need to skip your lure under the overhangs. Side-arm or underhand casting strokes, whether with plug, spin or fly tackle, provide a lower trajectory than the traditional overhand cast. Weedless jerkbaits and single-hook spoons work well in this situation, and an effective skip cast will cause a bait to fall in without much splash, and the reward may be an immediate strike.

Skip Casting

Pick a spot about a foot or so outside of overhanging cover. With a quick wrist snap, rodtip low to the water, cast toward that point. Try to hit the water at a nearly flat plane, so the lure "skips" back into the cover. With a spinning reel, use your forefinger to feather the line, or stop the lure cold before it skips too far. The technique works best with lightweight lures, especially smooth soft-plastic jerkbaits or plastic shrimp, weighting ¾ ounces or so. Because of the sharp acceleration required, the skip cast doesn't work as well with live baits, which may be slung off the hook. SB

A good skip cast sends a lure through a hole in the mangroves.

Drift Fishing

Though drift fishing is normally associated with big grassflats, the technique can be practiced in inlets and along beaches to pinpoint snook schools.

Here's a technique that inshore anglers somehow came to equate with seatrout. Yes, it is a great way to catch trout over a grassflat, but snook share the same flats, so what could be easier than allowing the current and/or wind to carry you along while you fan-cast or drag live baits along?

If fishing topwater plugs or soft plastics, it makes sense to cast either straight ahead or a 45-degree angle ahead of your drift where snook have not yet detected the boat. This is especially so in less than three feet of water. When either the tide or wind is so strong that you are pushed along briskly, casting straight ahead can require you to retrieve at too fast a clip. That's when it's best to quarter your casts slightly ahead, which allows you to fish them more thoroughly. When casting slow-sinking plugs, soft plastics (such as plastic shrimp) or light jigs, this allows the lure to sink to get near bottom.

Below, kayaker deployed a drift sock to slow his drift on a windy day.

If fly casting, the above advice also applies—cast slightly ahead of the drift. But be aware that with a floating line, during a fast drift, you may struggle with a pronounced bow in the line, a big curve, or belly, that makes it harder to manipulate the fly and to set the hook when the strike comes. For that reason, a slow-sinking line can be best. It will not form as big a belly, and even better, a sinking line does not collect floating seagrass. The speed of your drift may also dictate the sink rate of your fly. Remember that a sinking line and sinking fly will stay down in the water column best when the boat is moving.

To slow your drift on especially windy days, consider deploying a drift sock or drogue. When the sock fills with water astern, it acts as a brake, and you can fish lures more thoroughly.

A float signals a strike, gives you a visual of bait position and keeps a baitfish from reaching bottom. At left, anglers drift fishing over a pothole-pocked grassflat.

Live baits can be fished while drifting over the flats, too. Choose between freelining or fishing them under a popping cork. Live shrimp are a top choice year-round, and small whitebaits, finger mullet or pinfish can be deadly in summer. When dragged astern, give the cork a pop now and then. And add a splitshot or two when you are really sailing along to keep the baits down. A plastic shrimp is an option under a cork.

Passes and inlets are also ideal for drift fishing. Though there are times when anchoring is the local preference, drifting along with the current can be deadly at the edges of the main navigation channels. You can cast jigs, swimbaits and sinking plugs to dropoffs and quickly determine where bunched-up snook are holding in an inlet. Cast a jig ahead of your drift (downcurrent),

allow it to reach bottom, and then hop it along until it is upcurrent of the boat. By that time, it will have risen in the water, generally out of the reach of bottom-hugging snook.

Ideal casting angle is quartering ahead of a drifting boat's path. Another option is freelining or fishing a live bait under a float in the boat's wake.

Wind

Anchoring

Amid so many technological advances in boats and tackle, one piece of snook-fishing equipment remains largely unchanged—the anchor. Much of snook fishing involves current, and staying within range of some kind of structure. Whether you plan to soak livies

Florida Atlantic coast inlet snook taken on live bait. Anglers often anchor along dropoffs or over holes where snook are schooled.

around a jetty, toss flies at a dock light, or jig near a bridge or rivermouth, you'll want to hold your boat in place to give the spot the attention it deserves.

The first rule of anchoring a boat is to keep the bow of the boat pointed into the current. Water pushing against the flat transom will cause the boat to shift and bob, not the most comfortable or stealthiest option. When using claw-style anchors, a length of chain helps position the anchor in a better grabbing position and allows the use of a lighter anchor. To keep the hook in place, the scope should be about 6 to 1. That is, feed out 6 feet of anchor line for each foot of depth. Too much line can cause too much drift which can spook fish, and because your boat is shifting, decrease your casting accuracy. Sometimes, a

small second anchor near the transom can correct the situation.

There are three general factors to consider when anchoring: safety, distance from target and casting lanes. Since snook are commonly caught in high traffic areas and at night, the proximity to boating channels must be a consideration. Anchoring in a high volume channel not only jeopardizes the safety of the crew, but can be grounds for a ticket with hefty fines in some areas. Having to move your boat constantly because of oncoming traffic is no way to spend fishing time. Stay out of the way, and stay visible. Ensure that your anchor light is working and is clearly visible to other boaters from all angles.

Once the safety aspect of anchoring is addressed, determine a comfortable casting distance to your target. If casting flies or lures, that may be in the 35- to 60-foot range. If your hotspot has line-grabbing structure, you should consider your ability to control a big fish. If you set up too far away, especially when fishing mono or lines that have some stretch, you can bet a big snook will be around a piling three times, or 10 feet back into the mangroves, before you can stop her. If you are pinning big live baits to the bottom in deeper water near a bridge piling, distance is not as important as control. In this case, position the boat as close as needed to ensure accurate bait placement and an upper hand once the fish is hooked.

While at anchor, consider the direction in which snook will be facing—nose into the current.

ANCHOR SCOPE

Thinking of the bow of the boat as 12 o'clock, you should be casting a lure or fly at 10 or 11, or 1 to 2 o'clock if you cast left-handed, in order to retrieve with the current. On the other hand, live bait freelined or suspended under a float can be cast in just about any direction, as long as it drifts with the current to your likely strike zone.

Anchors can be particularly helpful from a canoe or kayak. A small mushroom anchor, attached via a trolley system, can allow paddlers to drift with the current and stop at each dock or other likely target long enough to get in a few good casts. To relocate, simply flip the little anchor into the boat, control your drift to the next spot and slide it back in.

In shallow water, say 4 feet or so, a pushpole or stick anchor deployed on a short line from the bow is handy for a temporary anchor.

Power-Pole deployed over hard sand bottom. Below, from top, kayak anchor, stick anchor and Danfoth anchor.

A six to one anchor scope should be used especially when anchoring in strong current over soft bottom.

Sight Fishing

Sight fishing for snook has grown tremendously in popularity, and can be practiced on tidal flats from spring through fall in the lower estuary, and over darker backcountry shallows in the dead of winter.

Angler looking for snook over dark mud bottom on a cool day. Warm sunshine draws snook to such shallows.

Bang the pushpole on the hull, or splash the tip in the water carelessly, and you'll see snook burst off the flat.

When stalking snook from a poling skiff, you must be in stealth mode. On windy days, you might get closer to snook you spot, but if your hull generates hull slap from the chop, it will put snook on alert. Many technical poling skiffs are quiet enough to eliminate this drawback. Snook do not normally plow across a flat like schooled reds, and don't grub in the bottom the way reds do. This fish tends to be a loner, and often "lays up," that is, takes a stationary position where it can ambush a meal. Potholes are great for this, as are the down-tide side of ridges, any slight depth change in fact. A snook's eyes are up; it's wary of predators. Snook can be as spooky as a big seatrout or a bonefish.

Your chances of spotting fish soar whenever there's good tide flow and ample forage around, especially on the skirts of flats close to safe, deep water. You must make a stealthy approach and then a good cast to ambush the great ambusher.

Carefully scan the back of any mudding rays you see, especially in water over 18 inches deep. Snook love to hide in the mud plume to pick off shrimp and baitfish, and even crabs. Make a cast or two over the back of a ray, and in the muddy water down-tide, even when you do not see a snook. You'd be amazed at how well they blend in.

It goes without saying that you must pole quietly. Bang the pole on the hull, or splash the tip in and out the water sloppily, and you may see a snook burst off the flat. When they do flee, they go in big spurts; unlike redfish, they rarely slow down right away and take a lure or bait. They must have better memories than redfish. Look for current slicks that mark depth changes. The slicks are over skinny water—and can be quite noticeable on windy days—the surrounding water is slightly deeper. And a slick can mark bait activity, so don't pass one by. Also look for potholes and debris such as dead wood.

During the winter, snook move inland to hunker down in deep holes in the backcountry. Some will ease up onto adjacent mud flats on warmer afternoons to soak up the sun over dark mud or shell bottom. These fish can really test your skills when the light is bright. Keep your distance when casting. And increase your sighting distance by stepping atop a cooler if your skiff lacks a bow casting platform. Invest in quality polarized glasses, and position yourself between the sun and your potential target. Facing the sun will significantly decrease your ability to see into the water. Wear subtle colored clothing. Just because fishing TV stars wear bright orange, pink or turquoise for the camera doesn't mean you should. Light blue, beige, khaki is a better bet. And in the backcountry where towering mangroves ring the shallows, drab olive gets the nod. Snook eyes have both rods and cones, suggesting they do see color.

PolingTip

Other than poling as quietly as possible, pole so that you don't make work out of it. Chances are you'll be on your favorite flat while the tide is moving. Don't work against the current unless you must do so to get the sun's glare out of your eyes. Rather, make the current work for you. Start a "pole-assisted" drift at the up-tide edge of a flat. Using the current as the main muscle, the pushpole should be used to steer the boat in the direction of likely snook hangouts—potholes, ledges, mangrove points and other prime lies.

Top, angler wears a hat with dark brim underside to reduce glare. Right, poling with the tip works over hard bottom, and the tip can be planted to hold boat.

Trolling

Trolling, once a mainstay method of snook fishing, remains a very effective way to find the fish. It may be just the ticket in blustery weather when it's tough to cast accurately. Lures that run at a particular depth can be helpful when trolling inlets, passes or manmade canals. In the mangrove backcountry, where every point looks as fishy as the next, trolling can zero you in on snook concentrations.

Most inshore rivers and coastal residential canals run from 7 to 10 feet deep. If you can find a ledge in the middle, that's the place to troll, especially in the winter. A spread of three big plugs—one deep-runner, one that runs at about four feet, and maybe a shallow-diver or suspending plug on top should cover the bases. This is

Trolliong can be just the ticket when snook are scattered.

Trolling along shore-lines will pinpoint concentrations of fish. Below, angler pulls an array of diving plugs close to bridge pilings.

an old-school approach to snook fishing. There are plenty of fishing articles from the '30s and '40s that tell fantastic stories of trolling Florida's estuarine rivers for tarpon and snook. The standard trolling lure was a No. 2 Drone Spoon, tied to a piece of light singlestrand wire to fend off abrasion from the snook's rough lips.

Trolling for big snook generally calls for medium-heavy to heavy tackle, certainly in the 15- to 25-pound class, with good line-to-line connections, hefty leaders and quality drag systems. The easiest approach at the larger bridges is to slow-troll plugs right along the shadowline, parallel to the bridge. Keep the first pass a few yards away from the shadowline so you can work your way closer without running over the fish. Troll the lure well astern because fish can be a bit wary of the boat. Weaving in and out of the pilings can cover prime holding lairs, but you have to respond quickly, and fish heavy tackle, to muscle hooked fish into the clear.

Kayaker trolling two lures under foot-pedal power.

Increasingly, kayakers are trolling artificials, either to keep fishing while paddling from spot to spot, or as a primary tactic. Snook are not readily alarmed by quiet kayaks, and you can paddle at whichever speed you choose to make a plug swim best or keep a jig at the right depth. Just make sure your rod holders are up to snuff. Remember to have ample 360-degree lighting if you choose to troll at night.

Trolling for snook takes a little planning. Since structure and dropoffs are ideal snook haunts, target such areas rather than trolling blindly in open water. Trolling parallel to mangrove shorelines can be effective. Higher tides allow for closer presentations practically under mangrove branches, but there's little argument that lower water is best, because your trolled lure will be spotted by snook that are flushed from the cover. In a shallow, mangrove-lined bay, there is often a strip of soft, bare mud between the mangroves and grassy flats. This natural transition can be a good place to troll when the water is too cloudy for sight fishing.

Above, specialized rod holder is ideal for hands-off trolling. Below, lipped plugs designed for various depths are ideal trolling lures.

When trolling multiple lures, be sure they swim at different depths to cover the water column.

Surf Snook

Walking the beach can be one of the most rewarding ways to fish for snook. It's ideal for the minimalist—a few jigs or flies in the pocket, one rod, and off you go. The first time a big snook belts your lure right at your feet and tears down the beach, you'll be hooked for life.

Casting parallel to the beach is the drill whether you sight cast or "prospect" fish.

After the spawn, big snook leave the inlets to feed in the surf.

This is hands-down the most popular and accessible sight fishery for the shore-based angler.

For the most part, late summer through early fall is prime time. After mild winters, a trickle of fish will show in April. But normally, mid-May is when the water hits the high 70s for good, and that's when surf snooking is worthwhile. The peak bite starts in late July, and the September bait run starts around the time many fish finish spawning, so it can be explosive.

Snook cruise the beach in singles, up to small groups of a half-dozen fish or so. Do not wade in waist-deep and cast to the horizon. Most snook swim within 20 feet of the sand. Parallel casting is the drill here, whether blind casting at first light or sight fishing later in the day. At low tide, many fish will have moved out toward the first bar, so try casting perpendicular to shore at that time.

Florida Gulf coast beaches adjacent to passes are thought to be spawning locations. Beach snook there tend to run in the 22- to 28-inch size, with the occasional large female in the middle of the group. On the Atlantic coast, they can be much, much larger along the surf.

Finding these fish is not difficult if you're willing to do some walking. Spend a little extra time scrutinizing any structure, like depressions, shell outcroppings or nearshore hard bottom. The Gulf coast beaches sometimes have downed trees, and that can be dynamite snook-holding structure. Snook are likely to take a breather at any relief along the shore.

If the beach is thick with bait, as is often the case during the summer and early fall, you're probably in business. When you see terrified, leaping bait or crashing birds, get to the spot and cast. During the mullet runs, snook tend to single this baitfish out. Other beach prey include bay anchovies, sardines, croakers, mojarra, whiting, and others. Many anglers catch bait on the spot, either with castnet or sabikis, and freeline the livies on a circle hook sized for the bait.

A good set of polarized glasses will help you spot fish, and you should dress in colors that blend in with the background. And be prepared to get on your knees when casting to snook in clear water right at your feet. The all-round beach snook rod for casting artificial lures is a 7½-foot spin or 7-foot casting rod that will cast jigs, weighted jerkbaits, and small topwater or suspending plugs in the ¼- to ½-ounce class. Once the fall mullet run com-

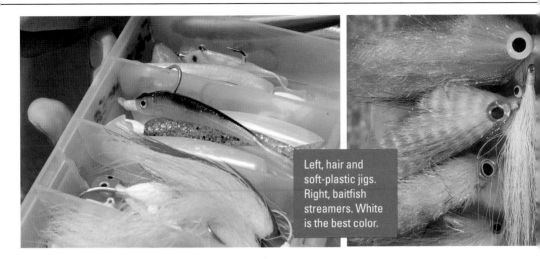

Left, hair and soft-plastic jigs. Right, baitfish streamers. White is the best color.

mences, you might beef things up a bit, both to battle the wind and lob bigger lures that entice the season's biggest beach snook. Avoid using snaps or snap swivels to connect line to leader or tie on lures—toothy blues and macks may be present and strike at such hardware. A bite leader of 30- to 50-pound monofilament or fluorocarbon is a must.

Fly fishers are happy to report that streamers can outfish all else in summer when small baits are on the snook's menu. When fall winds kick up, fly casting and line management can be a chore. If you beat the summer sunrise, a floating line and a popper such as the Crease Fly can score, but white, flashy streamers fished on a clear, intermediate sinking line is the bread-and-butter combination.

White, green-over-white and grey-over-white baitfish flies tied on No. 2 to 2/0 hooks are standard fare. Gulf coast flies tend to be smaller, with the Norm's Shminnow a regional favorite. Atlantic-side fly fishers like big Clouser Minnows and an array of greenie imitations. A sinking line is mandatory when there's wind chop, swell or seaweed in the water. Wear a stripping basket to keep line from underfoot. An 8- or 9-weight fly rod is ideal, though a 10-weight can handle big streamers that fish best in the fall. With a clear sinking line, leaders in the 4- to 6-foot range will suffice. But sight fishing for snook calls for a 9-foot or longer leader.

Fly casters target snook from summer through early fall. Stripping baskets keep line in order.

Flats Wading

Anglers squeamish about bailing out of a boat are missing out on the stealthiest of all methods of shallow-water snook fishing.

Wading is probably the single-most effective way to sneak up on a snook in shallow water. On slick calm summer mornings, skiff anglers, and even the quietest kayaker, would be wise to bail out and wade. Considering a snook's affinity for structure and ambush hunting, the best flats are those adjacent to mangrove shorelines, and those peppered with oyster bottom, sandy potholes, docks and other structure that provides cover for both snook and

Angler hooked this snook by wading waist-deep and casting back to shoreline cover.

baitfish. Blind casting over basically homogenous grass bottom can bag a snook but concentrating on such structure is more productive. Otherwise, cast where dissimilar grasses meet, at slight depth changes that are marked by slicks or choppy water, and naturally, where baitfish mark the surface.

Snook are not active cruising fish like redfish, but prefer to ambush-feed, like seatrout. Practiced waders fan-cast an area thoroughly before taking their next steps. And they shuffle their feet, to one, keep the noise down, and two, to protect themselves form stingrays. Shuffling kicks a ray up, and it normally scoots away. "High-stepping" is the best way to plunk a foot down on top of the animal, which back into you and barb you in self defense. Where the water is clear enough, scan for telltale signs of a partially buried ray—the top of the head and back normally show, or the sand bottom looks darker where the ray has recently settled into the

An early morning flood tide puts snook in the mood to corral baitfish in the shallows.

bottom. If you see a mud trail, that's an obvious warning to you.

As far as tackle for wading, choose a long spinning rod (7½ to 8 feet for example) with a soft tip to achieve maximum distance with lightweight lures and baits in the ⅛- to ¼-ounce class. Casting (plug) tackle is equally effective, however will perform best with slightly heavier jigs, spoons and plugs. The casting rods are normally shorter, between 6 and 7 feet, so might be more comfortable and accurate when you sidearm cast to fish spotted close by.

Even in the skinniest of water, be prepared to work the water column—jigs, suspending twitch or swimbaits, and topwaters all deserve space in your box. Fly fishers can mop up on the flats, particu-

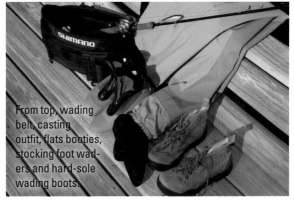

From top, wading belt, casting outfit, flats booties, stocking foot waders and hard-sole wading boots.

larly when snook are targeting smaller baits such as glass minnows or small shrimp. A fly rod will allow you to gently drop a small fly on a snook's nose. Wear a stripping basket to keep your line from underfoot and for easier shoots.

Deep Water

The battle started when a snook nabbed a live mullet soaked along a deep Everglades river shoreline.

Deep snook water can mean a 6-foot hole in a shallow back-country creek, or 30 feet or more in a major inlet or river.

Snook feed on the bottom quite a bit in the deepest water in creeks, rivers, bays, inlets or harbors. This occurs year-round though snook are a tropical fish. As a rule, snook will beat a path to the deepest rivers, basins and channels during the colder months, especially on the northern fringes of their range. Snook do not feed as aggressively in winter, and will even shut down for long periods when water temps stay in the mid 60s or lower.

Though you can't rule out an early arrival by Ol' Man Winter, the first significant cold fronts normally make it all the way through South Florida

in early December. That's when snook go into winter mode. Most move inland, heading toward the salinity barrier and sometimes beyond, and settle in or around deep holes that offer a bit of protection from the cold. A snook's metabolism slows, and the fish will stay deep until a string of warm days raises the water temp enough to prod it back to the shallows.

The best deepwater snook holes abut mangroves, mud flats, oyster bars, docks, or jetties and bridges. In winter, deep holes can be super producers if located in a lee and where they catch good afternoon sun. Extreme cold snaps send snook packing, and they will stack up in residential canals where the water may be salty, brackish or even fresh. If a deep hole is downtide of a shallow mud flat, it may catch sun-warmed falling water, an ideal scenario. Finally, if there are wading birds, birds of prey or alligators in the area you'll know there is prey on hand and quite possibly snook.

Everglades National Park backcountry waters have abundant deep holes that fish especially well in winter. Farther north along the Gulf coast every major river has deep holes in the headwaters that hold winter snook when the mouths are devoid of fish. The Myakka River has some fantastic holes up to 20 feet deep that hold winter snook, and on the Atlantic side, big snook are hooked in as much as 40 feet in Miami's Government Cut and Haulover

The deepest holes in a river can provide snook refuge in cold weather, a break from strong current and an ideal ambush site.

Inlet. Also, deeper reaches of most urban coastal canals from Biscayne Bay north to Canaveral, and the Loxahatchee, St. Lucie and Indian rivers are prime spots for deepwater snook.

Fish artificial lures slowly for winter snook in deep water. Retrieve as slowly as you can stand with a jig, swimbait or sinking plug. If live or natural baits are more your speed think about big live shrimp when whitebaits are scarce. Shrimp are most abundant in winter, and are precisely what snook tend to target when late winter-spring runs occur at the inlets and much of the lower estuary. Slow trolling with spoons, feathers, or plugs can be a shortcut to locating deep snook, after which you can anchor and work the area more thoroughly with the same lures. The Trol Rite is the universal lure/bait combo for deep snook year-round. It is simply a bare, ¼- to ¾-ounce teardrop-shape jighead, normally painted white or yellow. You "pin" a live shrimp to it, inserting the hook up through the head, avoiding the black brain. The combo is cast up or across current and bounced, or "rolled" along bottom.

Top, a snook from a wreck in 30 feet. Below, snook stacked over Goliath.

Fly fishing is not as widely practiced in deep holes, but fly fishers have success with lead core lines, and big, bushy shrimp flies or mullet patterns. A short leader will keep the fly level with the tip of the fly line, so that your fly stays as deep as possible. SB

Reef Snook

We know snook will hug the bottom of inlets and passes in some pretty deep water, and they are known to move to Florida Gulf reefs in up to 30 feet. On the Atlantic side, snook stack up on reefs and wrecks in 60 to 80 feet, with occasional reports of snook sightings from divers on wrecks as deep as 120 feet.

Anecdotal evidence suggests the numbers offshore are growing—enough to catch the interest of fisheries biologists.

"There seem to be more and more snook on reefs in the last 10 to 15 years," says Jim Whittington, marine biologist at the Florida Marine Research Institute. "What we don't know is what they are doing out there."

Many anglers assumed snook were moving off shore during the winter months to take advantage of the warm Gulf Stream waters. Researchers studying them had the opposite thought, they were zipping out during the summer months, possibly between spawning events. As it turns out, these fish might be out there most of the year, maybe even spawning out there.

Researchers have tagged some of these fish with acoustic "ping" tags, which track real-time movement of each fish tagged. The schools of snook lurking on the deep reefs and wrecks run large, as do the individuals. Although not really targeted, anglers have caught them while fishing for grouper and other reef fish. Biologists suggest that reef snook would benefit from venting, along with minimal handling. SB

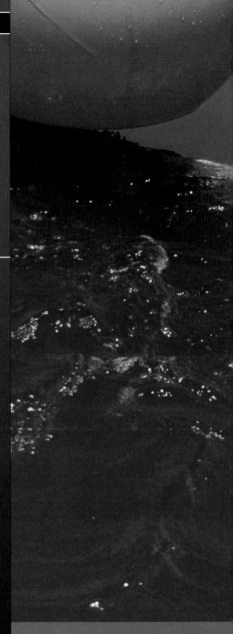

CHAPTER 11

Snook Structure

Discussing snook without mentioning structure would be like playing tennis without the ball. Veteran snook anglers rarely fish blindly in waters without some kind of structure.

It might be as subtle as a change in depth, or as obvious as a big bridge piling, seawall or commercial dock. In moving water, snook prefer to hang out where current carries food their way. Canals, cuts, and passes greatly increase the velocity of current—water is simply squeezed from a large area through a smaller space. Such natural and manmade contours will cause a break in flow, and sometimes you will notice a backflow or eddy, where water actually travels in the opposite direction of the main flow. Many types of prey are swept close to any structure in the water's path. Snook typically rest in the "sweet spot," the break in the current that structure provides, dashing out to ambush prey.

Veteran snook anglers rarely fish blindly in water without some kind of structure. It might be as subtle as a depth change or as big as a towering bridge.

See DVD for more tips on fishing snook structure.

This snook's 'hood has docks and bridges galore. Above, schooled snook glued to a rusting breakwater.

Mangroves

The red mangrove is identified by its arching prop roots; braced against the waves, this sturdy plant colonizes open shores.

Mangrove trees are the defining flora of snook habitat. If from a passing airliner you were to gaze down at the range of the common snook, you would see sparkling waters encircled by the green of mangrove crowns. Crossing these bays on an outboard-powered skiff,

Angler casts a lure back in the shadows in a hole in the mangrove roots.

your senses would be flooded by a sweet, sulphurous odor—as fallen leaves decay, the energy of the sun is converted into the foundations of a nutrient-rich ecosystem. Shady pockets beneath the root structure of the red mangrove offer shelter for juvenile snook; safe from porpoises, herons and other predators.

To survive in the salty tidal zone, mangroves evolved structures to process fresh water from salt, and to aerate the root systems. The red mangrove is identified by its long, arching prop roots; braced against the waves, this sturdy plant colonizes open shores. The black mangrove, typically found in calmer backwaters, bristles at its foundation with pencil-like pneumatophore roots, used as the name suggests, for exchanging air.

At the interface of ocean tides and freshwater sheetflow, red mangroves rooted in deep, peaty sediment may grow taller then 60 feet. These are the towering old trees of the Shark River in Everglades National Park, for instance.

Red mangroves inhabit Atlantic and Caribbean coastlines from peninsular Florida to Brazil. Hardy and impenetrable as they appear, mangroves are threatened by coastal residential and industrial development. The Florida development rush of the 1940s and '50s contributed to losses of as much as 87 percent of mangrove coverage in southeast Florida, and up to 59 percent in southwest Florida. Today, Florida has about 500,000 acres of mangrove forest and strict laws protecting these valuable trees.

The Everglades backcountry has thousands of miles of red mangrove shoreline at the water's edge; it all looks "snooky" but it's not. So how do you determine where to fish? First, determine whether that stretch of mangrove shoreline holds forage. Are there baitfish along the shoreline? Are there birds? Birds of prey don't waste much time in a wasteland. In the absence of birds, are the mangrove leaves splotched with white? That would be bird guano. So at least birds do frequent the spot from time to time. Is there tidal current? Finally, is there enough depth for snook at least during high tide? Is there a sharp undercut mud bank? If all of these conditions are present, you may have found a snook spot. And three out of four isn't bad!

When current flows tight against the roots of a red mangrove shoreline, you can expect a change

It appears to be low tide in this red mangrove labyrinth. Prop roots and oyster bars are exposed, making baitfish easy marks for snook.

in depth along the roots that protrude into the current, or the ends of a mangrove island that point in the direction of water flow. In other words, if the incoming tide is flowing toward the east, the western end of a mangrove island is likely to have a deep cut right at the base of the mangroves. Zoom past a spot like that in your skiff and you risk blowing past the best snook hole of the day.

A close inspection of such a channel or cut might reveal some other structure within that hole—a submerged log, mangrove branch or other debris. As water rips through that cut, expect snook to be waiting on the downcurrent side of the structure, waiting for prey washed by.

Which phase of the tide is best for mangrove snook in the mangroves? Most anglers prefer a low, outgoing tide because it forces snook and baitfish out of the root labyrinth. Further, there is more space between the lowest hanging branches and the water, an ideal opportunity to skip lures back into the cover where snook often lurk. At high tide, your only option may be to cast weedless soft plastics as deep as possible in the small nooks and crannies in the trees. Often, there is a strip of the flat just outside the mangroves that has relatively bare bottom. This strip can hold snook looking to warm up in the sun. Snook lurk right at the edge of the mangroves or the grass line for prey, too.

›PRO TIP Structure

Capt. Chris Myers

Specialty: Mangrove backcountry

Location: Mosquito Lagoon

Rod: Spinning, 7½-foot, medium power, fast action

Reel: Daiwa 2500 size spinning

Line: 10-pound poly braid

Leader: 30-pound fluorocarbon

Lure: D.O.A. Shrimp

Myers skips plastic shrimp under mangrove branches along shorelines that have quick dropoffs. "The best snook mangroves have deep water nearby, so the fish can take cover during extreme weather. Mangrove snook aren't necessarily large, but you have to turn them quickly—it only takes one barnacle encrusted prop root to slice your line."

Soft-plastic jerkbaits rigged weedless and plastic shrimp can be skip cast under mangrove canopy and into tight pockets, right.

There's reason to smile after winching a good snook from the mangrove jungle.

Along shallow mangrove shorelines, there is often a strip of relatively bare bottom where snook warm up on cold but sunny days.

Seagrass

To a shrimp a seagrass clump is a protective forest, and a baffle that catches detritus and allows it to settle to the bottom.

A feeding snook blasts its prey and turtlegrass from the surface. Right, angler scanning a Florida grassflat.

Seagrasses are critical to the entire aquatic food chain. The variety of shrimp, crabs, marine worms, baitfish and gamefish that depend on grassflats is astounding. Seagrasses are rooted in the ground just like terrestrial grasses, and thrive in areas of low turbidity and relatively low-energy waters. Strong currents and shifting bottoms make it difficult for roots to take hold. Dense patches of seagrass act as a baffle, which means they slow current. From the perspective of a small shrimp, a clump of turtlegrass is like a protective forest, bringing the slow currents above to a standstill and allowing particles and detritus to drift to the soft, protected bottom.

Needless to say, a big lush grassflat is heaven to snook and snook angler alike. But there are specific things to look for that help narrow down your search for snook. Pay special attention to margins where one type of grass abuts another. For example, turtlegrass growing at the deeper edge

of a flat will give way to the shorter, fine-bladed shoalgrass on the shallowest stretches that get high and dry at low tide. On a falling tide, snook hang at this margin to ambush baitfish following the falling water. Conversely, if you find a ribbon of turtlegrass running through a flat of shoalgrass, you now have a low-tide snook target, because the deeper turtlegrass indicates a deeper channel, a fish "funnel" where gamefish and prey can survive through a tide change.

If you find a ribbon of turtlegrass running through a flat of shoalgrass, you have found slightly deeper water and a low-tide snook spot.

From left, skimmer jigs, jerkbait, weedless spoons and plastic shrimp. Below, weedless flies.

Catch Snook, not Weeds

A lush grassflat is highly productive in both the forage and predator departments, but can be a tough place to fish with artificials.

You can't retrieve many lures through heavy grass. If your hook is adorned with even a small strand, that is enough to ruin the action, or tip a snook off that something's amiss. The key is to guard the hook, or bury it in the lure. At the least, you want a lure that rides hook-up.

Weedless spoons, skimmer (a.k.a. bonefish) jigs, numerous soft-plastic jerkbaits and plastic shrimp, and fly patterns with built-in mono or wire weedguards that imitate baitfish, crabs and shrimp are all good artificials for grassy flats.

And it helps to retrieve any of this assortment with your rodtip above your head. That way, you can skim your lure along over the tips of the grass, and perhaps allow it to flutter down into the jungle or a bare pothole from time to time.

For snook you'll need to tie a 20- to 40-pound-test monofilament or fluorocarbon bite leader to your lure, so go with the slimmest knot possible to avoid catching bits of grass or algae. SB

Seagrass Menu

Turtlegrass grows in meadows that are the densest in inshore waters, providing refuge for essential snook prey.

Year-round seagrass prey species for snook include gobies (family Gobiidae), blennies (family Blenniidae), and some species of wrasse (family Labridae). Most are relatively small (generally less than four inches), so are potential prey items for even the smallest snook. These baits live on bottom and seldom surface. They live among grass blades, drift algae and in shells. Gobies and blennies rest on bottom when not feeding, and dart about with short, rapid movements. Small jigs can be used to imitate these relatively small baits, and there are dozens of good fly patterns (both impressionistic and realistic) that work well for snook.

Killifish (family Cyprinodontidae) inhabit subtropical, grassy shoreline shallows year-round. These 1- to 4-inch fish are brassy olive in color and are relished by snook.

Grassbeds, turtlegrass particularly, are restaurants for snook.

Shoalgrass (thinner blades at left) and turtlegrass (three wide blades at right) are flat-bladed, as is eelgrass (not pictured). Shoalgrass grows on the shallowest shoals and tolerates long-term air exposure better than turtlegrass. Below, turtlegrass tends to be sparser close to red mangrove shorelines.

Pinfish are an essential prey species in subtropical and warm-temperate seagrass beds. Size, abundance and habitat use changes seasonally. Pinfish larvae enter estuaries and seagrass flats in the winter. These larvae then transform into juveniles less than an inch long that have all features of an adult. Juvenile pinfish prefer seagrass beds that contain drift algae, which provides both food and shelter. A pinfish less than an inch long in March will be a couple of inches long by summer.

As pinfish grow, they become a staple prey for snook. Snook in southwest Florida, for example, seem to prefer pinfish from 1½ to 5 inches long. Pinfish fly patterns are common, and as for lures, many crankbaits fairly imitate pinfish. Many shrimp and crabs reside in seagrasses. Brown and white shrimp are common, as are blue crabs. SB

Other Natural Structure

Sandbars can be great stopping points during a snook fishing trip. They are formed by, and interact with, fast moving water and sometimes conflicting currents. Often, the outside of a pass or inlet is braced by intermittent sandbars.

Because these bars interfere with the flow of water, they create eddies and sheltered pockets, and can funnel water (and prey) into a tighter area—an ideal snook-holding spot. But sandbars are by no means permanent. They can shift, increase in size or length, or slowly erode away. However, after a significant weather event such as a hurricane, a sandbar can be completely excavated. Conversely, new bars commonly form after a storm and can remain in place for years. Regardless of why and how long it is there, a sandbar can be a very worthwhile visit when searching for snook.

Because sandbars form in high-energy areas, they don't normally have dense seagrass growth. If they do have grass, it may be "stunted" a bit. For example, turtlegrass may not be as long and lush as what you may find over a protected, sand-bottom shoreline flat.

A mud flat is a common backcountry feature. The best mud flats for snook aren't necessarily hundreds of yards wide. Fish typically relate to a transition between the relative safety of mangrove roots during high

A buffet line of sorts forms where tidal current squeezes through a breach in a sandbar. Cast lures upcurrent of snook-holding spots.

SAND BAR

TIDAL FLOW

BAIT FISH

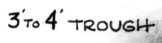

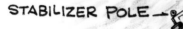

SAND BAR

STABILIZER POLE

This angler is navigating spoil island sandbars via electric motor while casting to dropoffs.

tide, or the deep channel during low tides and periods of extreme weather. During the winter, dark mud flats are great sight fisheries for snook. The fish slide up from deeper channels late in the morning, looking to soak up as much of the sun's warmth as possible. The early arrivals may be there just to warm up, but in time may feed with abandon.

The mouths of creeks or rivers, whether they empty into a bay or open ocean, can be outstanding snook holes. Usually, the depth across a wide rivermouth is not constant. Find the deeper holes and you are looking in the right spots for snook, especially in cold weather or at low tide. Conversely, humps on the bottom, whether rock or shell, create an edge for snook to rest behind out of the fastest current.

Expect to find snook over both sandbars and softer mud bars whenever baitfish school over them. At high tide, baitfish will seek relative refuge from predators in deeper water nearby. However, a snook may be more tuned into bottom forage here. A snook will not hesitate to scoop up a burrowing crab, snapping shrimp or similar crustaceans that call sandbars home.

Sandbars provide excellent footing, but mud flats or bars typically are too soft for wading.

Sandbars on Charts

On nautical charts, sandbars, like oyster bars and similar shoaling, are depicted by green shadings a bit darker than the yellow color of the land masses. Normally, sandbars will run parallel to current, such as extensions of the ends of spoil islands, which like the Intracoastal Waterway, run north and south. If a sandbar on a chart has a dotted line as a border, that means that the bar uncovers on lower stages of the tide. Also, the letter S may be marked to indicate sandy bottom. Be aware that sandbars can be washed out or built overnight by storms. So don't depend on a chart as your sole aid to finding bars. SB

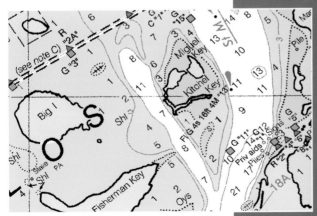

Oyster Bars

The role of oysters is crucial to a body of water. A healthy live oyster bed is a super water cleanser; in fact a single oyster can filter as much as a gallon of water each day! Oyster bottom is also terrific snook fishing habitat. It attracts baitfish and assorted crustaceans, and an oyster bar provides ambush points for snook. An oyster mound may be the only structure on a mud flat, and can be the only place to find snook. Some oyster mounds are a few feet in diameter; others can be many yards across. But a mature, live bed of oysters can rise up high enough that you may see oysters drying above the waterline for the entire bottom third of a tide. If you see the top of an oyster mound at high tide, you can bet the base is quite wide. A cluster of oysters grows out as well as up, to help spread the weight and stay "afloat" on soft mud.

Deep holes are often scoured out by the current

Nearshore Hard Bottom Hard bottom on the beach close

Snook often forage along beaches from mid-summer through fall, often in ankle-deep water. They target a wide array of baitfish that migrate in the trough. However, you can find more fish over nearshore hard bottom than over otherwise featureless beach bottom. And chances double if the hard bottom is within a mile of an inlet.

Florida's southeast coast has numerous stretches of nearshore hard bottom, and during the summer spawning period it can produce some fast early morning snook fishing. Snook can spawn as often as every 2 or 3 days throughout the summer, so they will eat ravenously to maintain the energy reserves needed.

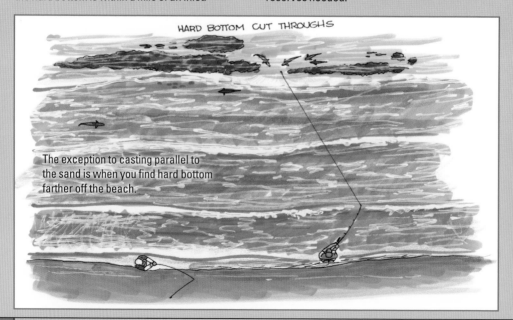

HARD BOTTOM CUT THROUGHS

The exception to casting parallel to the sand is when you find hard bottom farther off the beach.

Most oyster bars uncover at low tide. Left, bar jutting from the shoreline may be sight fished at high tide.

bars for not only food, but warmth. Dark shells and mud soak up the sun's heat, though smaller bars surrounded by deep water may not provide a snook much relief from cold water.

But the water temp in a shallow bay or creek with numerous oyster bars can rise appreciably on sunny winter days, putting the fish in a feeding mood.

Fishing for snook over oyster bottom can be tricky. First of all, shell bottom can

on the uptide end of an oyster bar. Snook and other fish typically line up to feed in such holes at one tide phase or another.

During winter, snook are attracted to oyster

slice your line or leader, especially when under tension during a snook fight. At the very least, oyster can abrade your line, so it pays to check it repeatedly while fishing.

You can pole over oyster bars at high tide, but it's best to use the tip rather than the foot of the pushpole. Even then, you must be careful not to push with too much might. The tip could slip,

to inlets can be a snook goldmine.

Nearshore reefs are home to hundreds of species of fish, shrimp, crabs, and other snook prey. Mojarra are a primary snook forage species, as are spottail pinfish. Juvenile snapper and grouper linger around these structures when they are about the size of your thumb, and hang around until they are large enough to move out to the next tier of reefs in about 20 to 30 feet of water. Many of these reefs on Florida's Atlantic coast are "worm rock" and are referred to as biogenic because worms build the reef. As they grow, the solid base serves as a platform to which various corals attach, adding to the biodiversity of the system. Snorkelers are often treated to the sight of small schools of snook that cruise the reefs in search of a baitfish breakfast. SB

Angler probing for snook along exposed worm rock reef.

and so could you, right off the tower to sharp shells below. Be careful not to "clang" the shell bottom with a pole too much. It will send out a warning to any snook in the vicinity. A trolling motor can be run if the water is deep enough, but one ding of the blade on shell will send snook running. It goes without saying that lures that are relatively weedless, such as spoons, Texas-rigged soft baits and skimmer jigs are best over shell. You may be better off fishing topwater plugs, or best yet, a soft plastic, live shrimp or baitfish suspended below a popping or rattling float.

Whenever possible, cast from a distance so as not to alarm snook.

Manmade Structure

If man builds it, snook will come. And that is no joke. Manmade structure is easy to find because most or at least part of it is above the waterline. It's not like you have to find some submerged, secret junk. Though that may be the case with debris that results from bridge or dock building.

Docks, seawalls, bridges and jetties are top spots for snook and the prey they eat. These structures also provide a break from current, refuge from apex predators, and terrific venues from which to launch an attack. Also, a great place to sever a fishing line.

Docks

Adult snook exhibit a high degree of adaptability, and commonly gravitate to docks and other manmade structure. Though many anglers equate docks with lights and the dark of night, they do hold snook during the day so long as there is forage

Dock pilings provide snook refuge as well as a prime ambush station.

around. During daylight hours, snook lurk in the shadows out of the direct sun. Often they sit just inside the shadowline, facing the current, peering into the lighter waters waiting for a meal while enjoying the relative safety of cover. Though snook will venture out of a dock's shadows at night to feast on prey attracted to lights, you'll find that skipping baits and lures far under a dock is the key to catching fish during the day. It is also necessary to fish deeper under docks during the day, unless bait schools are passing through at the surface. Many snook anglers swear by old, dilapidated docks. Those that are "out of service" are best due to the lack of foot traffic. Also, such docks normally have lots of marine growth, which attracts small fish which attract snook. On the flip side, docks in use may be lighted, making it a top night spot. If a boat is tied up for extended periods, snook use the hull as an extension of the dock. A sailboat at a dock signifies that the water is deep, which big snook prefer.

Angler displays a fine specimen that struck along a residential canal seawall.

Seawalls

If you've ever seen a cops-and-robber movie you've seen the police corner the crooks in a dark alley and slam them up against a wall.

That is exactly the way snook use seawalls to grab a meal. Seawalls are like a one-way street for mullet or any other baitfish rising with the current. Snook will patrol seawalls in packs, much

like jack crevalle, and rush baits to the surface. The carnage can be impressive. Where seawalls meet in a close corner, the outcome is not good for the mullet. Wherever seawalls form a corner that juts out into a channel or inlet, an eddy will form on the down-tide side, and that tends to hold baitfish, shrimp and crabs. That is a classic ambush point for snook. They get easy meals and a break from the brunt of the flow.

Fishing seawalls is easy for anglers on foot. As you would when fishing the surf, you simply cast parallel to the wall. When snook are visibly busting bait on the surface, topwater or subsurface lures are best. Otherwise, try a jig or lipped sinking plug. Boaters can anchor off a seawall, or move along while casting via electric motor.

Keep in mind that many seawalls have mounds of riprap (boulders) at their base, and this may not be visible at high tide. You'll need to keep a hooked fish from reaching the debris.

When the winter water temps are borderline for snook comfort, a long and preferably dark seawall can radiate the sun's heat by midafternoon. This may be an actual snook sauna on the coldest of days.

Many Florida bridges have excellent catwalks, some of which are lighted for night fishing. Below, bridges in city centers often provide the sole structure for snook.

Bridges

Bridges that span inlets, passes, rivers and Florida's Intracoastal Waterway are prime snook spots. Bridges tend to attract big specimens, due to the refuge they provide in relatively deep water with strong current. Strong current over time scours deep holes at the bases of the pilings, where snook hunker to escape the brunt of current and ambush passing prey. Bridges over wide waterways may see a huge push of water at mid-tide. Sometimes better

fishing can be had at tide changes, when it's easier to present baits and position the boat.

Fishing can be done from a bridge if walkways are provided on the bridge itself or there are catwalks beneath the bridge. There is a point of no return regarding bridge height. The easiest bridges to fish from are low to the water. Even though this

is largely "vertical" fishing because snook often hang directly under the bridge, a big belly can form in your line due to current and even high winds. That can spoil your presentation with either live baits, jigs or plugs. Then there is the matter of getting your hooked snook to hand.

On bridges where fishing from atop is prohibited, and there are no catwalks, your only option is to fish from a boat. Such a bridge gives you lots of water to work because there are no fishing lines dangling from above. Anchoring just uptide of a bridge allows for the freelining of live baits, bottom-bouncing with jigs, and casting sinking plugs parallel of the span. If the bridge has lights, a distinct shadowline forms, and the fish will station themselves in the dark water just downtide, very close to the pilings. Whether you anchor up or use an electric trolling motor for more mobility, be sure that you are keeping your bait or lure in this productive zone. At times, snook will be visible in the light or busting baits on top. Otherwise, the fish will hang deeper in the water, and may even sulk on bottom close to pilings and abutments when the tide slows.

Over time, current scours out depressions around bridge pilings which snook occupy during peak flow.

Anglers team up to land a Fort Pierce jetty snook.

anglers opt out of fishing the spawners. The relief of the jetty itself provides shelter for multitudes of bait, snapper and grouper of various sizes, and shellfish from the tiniest of shrimp to giant lobsters. Opportunistic snook can find some prey or another pretty much year-round. Dedicated jetty anglers literally camp out on the jetties, fishing where the depressions and riprap along the bottom hold the most promise. Snook are often holding right at the bottom, tight to the jetty, where the water is flowing slower.

In the fall, Florida gets nor'easters that generate gigantic surf along the Atlantic coast. In that case, surf fishing is out of the question, and even the mouths of inlets (particularly on a falling tide) can be dangerous for boaters. However, jetties on the northern side of inlets provide a break from the seas. That can be the only place where shorebound anglers can fish for snook. (Sebastian Inlet is a prime example.)

Jetties

Jetties are the place to fish in most inlets. This is largely a summer fishery because of the sheer numbers of spawning fish that congregate either in or adjacent to most inlets. In Palm Beach Inlet, for example, the south jetty normally holds a massive ball of snook almost all summer long, though many

Anglers should consider their personal safely, because jetties vary in fishability. Some having hard, paved walkways and rails, and others are more primitive and downright dangerous for foot traffic under stormy conditions. See chapter 15, Snook Hotspots, for more specific information on Florida jetty conditions. SB

Snook hug the rocks on high water but move out to sandy bottom on low tides.

CHAPTER 12

Spillways

The saying, "timing is everything," can apply to fishing in general, but especially to fishing spillways. These manmade barriers between fresh and salt water can be found on just about every canal in South or Central Florida. And they produce some terrific snook fishing when the gates first open, which depends on actual rainfall, or expectations of heavy rainfall. When water managers decide to dump fresh water into the ocean, or "to tide" as they say, anglers who drop everything and get to the spillways enjoy fast fishing. So, ironically, some the fastest snook fishing in Florida is triggered by man.

Spillways have had a significant impact on the development of South Florida. In the early 1900s, most of them were fixed lock structures that opened or closed to permit barge and boat passage. Produce and other tradable goods were ferried from the south-central part of the state through the locks and shipped around the country. Eventually, highways replaced the need for such water transit, and most locks and dams were converted into spillways to allow for the reclamation of wetlands during the development boom, or to keep farms dry during the rainy season.

Disoriented and sometimes injured prey tumbling in the wash are an easy mark for opportunistic snook and other predatory fish that come to the dinner bell.

S48

DANGER
NO
SWIMMING
WITHIN 500 FT.

The author with a
bright spillway snook.
Light coloration
suggests the fish
just arrived from the
lower estuary.

Snook Magnets

Some spillways can be fished from a boat, some have limited bank access, and a few have dedicated piers for fishing.

Spillway gates typically open from the bottom, and depending on the degree to which the gates are raised, can allow a trickle or huge slug of fresh water to flow to the seaward side of the structure. Unfortunately, massive dumps can lower the salinity of the estuary to destructive levels in a short time (not to mention introduce pollutants and silt which harm or bury all marine life). Shad, bluegills, cichlids, speckled perch, golden shiners, catfish, mullet and crawfish are flushed downstream of the structures, through a gauntlet of turbulence and turbidity. Disoriented and sometimes injured prey is an easy mark for op-

Here's five feet of angler and four feet of snook. This spillway giant took a live bait and was released.

portunistic snook, tarpon, jacks, ladyfish and other predatory fish which use the dirty water to their advantage to ambush a meal.

Once a spillway is closed, snook that came

running for the initial dinner bell should remain in the vicinity of the structure as long as the forage remains. However, the intensity of the feeding will greatly subside. Eventually, if the gates remain closed on a spillway—particularly if close to the coast and salt water—the salinity rises and any remaining freshwater baitfish perish.

Spillway Techniques

Not all spillways are equally angler-friendly. Some can only be fished from a boat, while others limit the number of shore-bound anglers, or have steep, treacherous shorelines. Some have dedicated fishing piers which allow for ideal casting angles, not to mention safe footing.

For example, Florida's Lake Worth spillway, located in Palm Beach County, is a top snook structure, but you can't fish it effectively from a boat. The boat barrier cable (marked by floating buoys) is too far downstream of the structure to allow anglers to cast to the main flow where snook congregate. However, there are excellent fishing piers along both canal banks close to the action.

At spillways where boat fishing is allowed, a whole new set of challenges arises. First, since it is illegal to tie off to the barrier cable line, anglers must ease the nose of the boat up on to the cable, and anchor as close as possible. Another option is, with the motor in idle and forward gear, allow the hull to make contact with the cable just enough to keep the boat in place. With the boat securely in place, your casting lanes should be wide open as long as you aren't sharing the space with 15 other boats shoulder to shoulder. Should you hook a snook upcurrent of the cable, and the fish powers its way downstream, you may have to reach down and pass your rod under the cable, which is not as easy as it sounds.

Pick spillway tackle that would suffice for big snook at a pier or bridge. You'll also need a lifting device to get your fish from the water to hand at spillways that can't be fished from a boat or on foot right at the water's edge. Spin or conventional tackle in the 12- to 20-pound class is standard at spillways, with the emphasis on backbone. You want a medium-stiff, fast-action rod with power to spare in the butt to move a big snook in strong current. Not pool-cue stiff—that would not allow you to feel the sometimes subtle taps of snook taking lures off

For a natural spillway presentation from a boat, cast straight upcurrent or at a 45 degree angle.

the bottom. A reel's line capacity is not a major concern in such close quarters. But its smoothness is important; a herky-jerky drag means lost fish. A high retrieve ratio will help greatly when a fish changes directions and rushes toward you with the current. You can normally get away with extra-heavy bite leader, too. Consider 50-pound fluorocarbon or monofilament as a minimum. At night, you might get away with a short trace of light wire—something to consider when chucking those $15 magnum plugs.

The Gatekeeper Schedule

The South Florida Water Management District oversees spillways located on the Florida east coast from Fort Pierce south and on the Gulf coast as far north as Lee County. For spillway locations and the latest spillway conditions, visit my.sfwmd.gov and click on "Water Conditions" to get real-time data describing water flow volume at spillways.

The Southwest Florida Water Management District controls canal levels and water discharge schedules from the Tampa Bay area north to Levy County. For spillway information in this region, visit www.swf wmd.state.fl.us. Click on "Data & Maps" and then click "Structure operations hydrologic report." SB

Snook find easy pickings in the most turbulent outflow below open spillway.

Artificial Lures

You may be inclined to think that artificial lures would be ignored around a spillway that is gushing and flushing hundreds of live baitfish to awaiting snook. But lures do work well, both day and night, because the water is

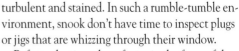

Left, good spillway lures include walking plugs, lipped divers, and plastic jigs, and at right, heavy hair jigs.

turbulent and stained. In such a rumble-tumble environment, snook don't have time to inspect plugs or jigs that are whizzing through their window.

Before selecting a lure, factor in the force of the flow, water clarity, time of day and the forage on hand. Most veteran spillway anglers cast suspending or sinking lures, with jigs, soft-plastic weighted swimbaits and fast-sinking plugs most popular when the spillway flow is especially strong. But a topwater plug can take snook wherever there is a large eddy that gives snook and baitfish a break from the current, or when the flow is minimal. Also, topwaters fish well along the canal banks well downstream of the structures.

Most spillways have manmade rip-rap bottoms that are designed to control erosion when water is

▶PRO TIP

Capt. Danny Barrow
Specialty: Spillways
Location: Lake Worth, Florida
Rod: Conventional rated for 15- to 25-pound line, with a heavy power rating
Reel: Shimano Curado 300 DSV
Line: 40-pound poly braid
Leader: 50-pound fluorocarbon
Lure: Heddon Super Spook

Barrow uses heavy tackle for good reason. "I want to land the big fish, not leave a lure in the snook's mouth as she swims away," says Barrow. "My lures are oversize, too, so beefy rods allow me to cast them for distance and accuracy, and manipulate them in heavy current."

The Heddon Super Spook is Barrow's go-to spillway plug, and he advises anglers to change colors to get the bite. When the snook run large, he often upgrades his stock treble hooks to 3X or 4X No. 2 and Owner Hyper Wire No. 4 split rings.

"Get that fish turned your way immediately," says Barrow. "A big snook in spillway current needs to make short runs. Clamp down on your drag and she'll break your heart."

ripping through. Snook like to hide within this relief, so swimming your bait as close to the bottom as possible makes sense. Soft, single-hook lures that resemble a shad are a fine start. If you are partial to hard baits, avoid divers with huge lips—you will continually hang bottom.

The ½- to 1½-ounce flare hawk jigs so popular with bridge anglers work well at spillways. White-and-red or chartreuse are typical colors. This lure might be responsible for more gigantic spillway snook than any other. This impressionistic jig's bushy reverse-tied skirt makes for a big profile, which serves well in turbid water or at night. Snook take it for a big baitfish.

Smaller jigs can be just as deadly at a spillway. Matching the jig body to the right size and style head is critical here—control of your lure will make the difference between a few lucky fish and a memorable bite. During times of very heavy flow, increase the weight relative to body size. The most effective use of smaller jigs is working along the rocky bottom, in the same direction as the water flow. Braided line is very helpful because of the need to distinguish between a bottom bump and a lunker's thump. Work the jig close to the bottom with a medium-heavy rod, and hold the tip high in the air to decrease the chance of hanging up.

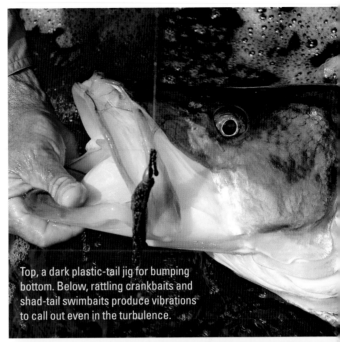

Top, a dark plastic-tail jig for bumping bottom. Below, rattling crankbaits and shad-tail swimbaits produce vibrations to call out even in the turbulence.

With sinking lures, the basic approach is to cast upcurrent, close to the structure, and then let it sink to bottom. Then swim it along while raising and lowering the rodtip. Fish hit as it gets downstream of you, too. And be prepared to get "whacked" as it swims back to you from across the canal.

Fly fishing can be problematic at spillways when they are flowing strong. Even with sinking lines, it's tough to get flies down deep. But the real problem is backcasting room, though there is the possibility of roll casting a shooting head from the surface for short presentations. There are smaller water control structures more conducive to fly casting, however. For example, the Tamiami Trail canal in the Miami area, as well as in Southwest Florida close to Naples, has several culverts, and there are many weirs in suburban canals near Naples that hold snook. Small streamers can be deadly here, and baby tarpon often crash the snook party.

Angler fished from behind the rail of an extended spillway wall to nail this over-size snook.

Spillway regulars who livebait fish opt for medium-heavy conventional or spinning tackle to keep hooked fish out of bottom rip-rap, clumps of mangroves or adjacent fishing piers, and finally, the spillway barrier cable.

Freelined live baits call for big circle hooks because most of the snook caught will be overslot size. Long leaders (five or more feet) in the 60- to 80-pound-test class are best, and many anglers spool up with 25-pound mono as a minimum, or braid in excess of 30-pound test. If you find the right eddy, you can present a freelined bait and keep it there for long periods; otherwise be prepared to make several casts to keep your bait in the target area for as long as possible. If you are fishing from a boat, do not let your bait drift under the cable, or the snook that catches you off guard might just be leaving with your tackle.

Though spillway snook will eat just about any bait with fins and a tail, remember to check regulations regarding the use of live finfish as bait. Don't castnet in fresh water for small panfish, and never transport live invasive fish from one body of water to another. It's flat-out illegal, and some of the tempting baits like cichlids can survive in brackish water below a spillway.

Smaller live baits freelined at a spillway might draw a lot of strikes, but increasing your landing percentages will require a lot of practice and finesse. Sometimes you will need to make considerably long casts to get bait to the prime ambush site. Throwing small baitfish for any distance with a stiff baitcasting outfit is hard to do. The only solution is to go to a longer, softer spinning rod. However, this can be a tradeoff that can backfire should you hook a real dinosaur that is intent on making a head-long surge to the nearest bottom debris or that big cable just downstream. SB

Live Bait

The key to fishing live baits during strong spillway discharges is to ensure that you present them naturally. Choose between freelining baitfish and pairing them with a jighead. With the latter method, you can cast a large live bait and get it deeper, then slowly retrieve it to cover maximum water.

Residual Effects

Sometimes you can fish a spillway indirectly. Usually a spillway canal feeds an estuary or perhaps the Intra-coastal Waterway. When the structure has been releasing fresh water for days on end, the spillway fishing can cool off. That's when snook, tarpon, jacks and other fish will move to the mouth of the spillway canal. Casting to the shorelines or any seawalls in the immediate area can pay off. SB

Five of Florida's Best Spillways

S-80: St. Lucie Canal (C-44)

This structure is a combination lock/spillway that serves both to allow boats through to Lake Okeechobee and to discharge water at the whims of the SFWMD. Located just west of the FL Turnpike, just north of S.R. 76. Large structure that can be fished from boat or on foot.

S-29: Snake Creek Canal (C-9)

A productive spillway when water is really moving. Located just east of U.S. 1, north of Hwy. 820. Boat access and canal directly downstream of spillway has a small fishing pier.

SR-29-1: State Road 29 Canal

Southernmost weir on the canal along S.R. 29, just west of Turner River where it crosses the Tamiami Trail (S.R. 41). Can be approached best by canoe or kayak, but plenty of anglers fish the canal near the trail on foot.

S-79: Caloosahatchee River

The lock/spillway combination that connects Lake Okeechobee to the Caloosahatchee in Southwest Florida. Located just north of S.R. 80. The structure and its fishable downstream waters are accessible by boat only.

S-155: Palm Beach Canal (C-51)

This major spillway controls water levels for vast areas of land. During dry periods, might not open after locally heavy rains. During wet periods, may remain open for months. Located on Lake Worth/West Palm Beach border, just west of U.S. 1. Fishable only from piers (no boat access).

This spillway pier allows for upcurrent casts and plenty of elbow room.

Other popular spillways in Palm Beach County include the Earman River Spillway, in North Palm Beach. This one permits walk-in fishing and fishing from a boat, and has two piers. South of that is the Lake Worth Spillway, on the West Palm Beach Canal. This spillway can only be fished from shore, as barrier barrels hundreds of yards downstream of the structure shut out boats. Other structures

can be fished on the C-16 Canal in Boynton Beach; the C-15 at Boca Raton; and the Hillsboro Canal, in Deerfield Beach. All three are more suitable for boat fishing. A spillway at Pompano Beach, near Palm Aire, is on the C-14 Canal. Dade County's Snapper Creek Spillway, located in Coral Gables, is just upstream of Snapper Creek's mouth south of Matheson Hammock in Biscayne Bay. SB

Moderate flow such as this may precede or follow a stronger water release.

CHAPTER 13

Night Fishing

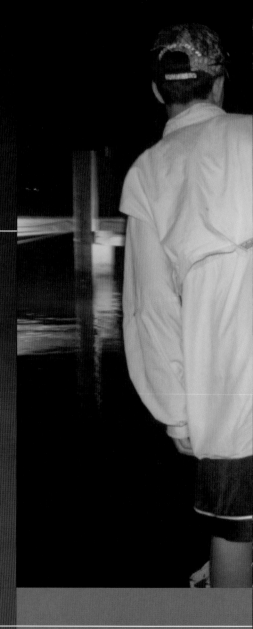

Many snook anglers have scored their biggest fish at night. But the prospect of nailing a trophy is just part of it. There is just something about fishing under the stars on an inky black night, or by the glow of a full moon, with the knowledge that a big snook is prowling that bridge span, the shadow under a dock or the eddy just behind the jetty tip. Your senses are heightened. Every pop and splash puts your hairs on end.

She's eyeing my lure right now, you tell yourself.

So you fish more intensely, more intuitively, more thoroughly. Unlike during the day, distractions are few. It's just you and the snook, and maybe a buddy, while the rest of the town's asleep.

Rather than lying awake all night wondering why the day's snook fishing was tough, fanatical snookers head out well after the sun goes down.

See DVD for more on docklight fishing.

Right, an outstanding flyrod bridge catch. Florida bridges produce bigger snook on average than lighted docks, top.

The Nighttime Advantage

Many snook fishermen believe the bite is better at night. Some anglers claim that 9 of 10 snook are caught after the sun goes down. And that might not be far from the truth. Snook is the number one nighttime inshore fishing target in South Florida waters, with tarpon getting a few votes. Not very many anglers drag themselves out of bed in the wee hours, or do all-nighters, to catch redfish or trout.

A snook's eyes are excellent for night feeding.

So they are simply good night hunters.

It is not hard to imagine why snook fishing is better at night. Less boat traffic factors in, and in the shallowest water, the cloak of darkness takes the edge off otherwise wary fish. You can expect to catch snook at night in all of the places you catch them during the day. Though few anglers take to the beaches at night, tossing plugs and jigs in the surf can be excellent. Full moon periods are easiest to fish because you can see what you are doing under moonlight. Many beginners are surprised to discover that snook fishing is excellent in pitch black in passes and inlets. Veteran inlet snookers have long taken trophy fish on big jigs and live baits fished right on the bottom.

But there is no denying that the most popular snook fishing occurs around artificial light.

There's no denying that the most popular night snook fishing occurs around artificial light.

A snook watches for passing prey under a submerged dock light.

Snook are readily drawn to lights where they ambush bait-fish of all descriptions, shrimp and small crabs. Lighted docks and bridges are hands down the most productive nighttime snook fisheries when it comes to numbers. Snook patrol the shadowlines provided by bridg-es, and similarly, lights under a dock. But these two structures differ somewhat. Whereas bridge-light shadowlines primarily give snook a corridor in which to ambush prey in the darkness just downtide of lighted water, dock lights set up a miniature food chain that attracts prey and preda-tor alike. Whether a dock has overhead or underwater lights, the light attracts phytoplank-ton (minute aquatic plants) that are the primary forage for zooplankton (animal plank-ton), which are in turn eaten

They are high on the fish's head, allowing the fish to look up for prey swimming above. More impor-tantly, snook eyes have a layer of cells covering the retina that aid in the gathering of ambient light.

by tiny shrimp, crabs and baitfish of all sizes. It's no wonder that snook, as well as seatrout, tarpon, ladyfish, lookdowns and others come to the lights at night.

DOCK TIPS

1) Avoid the slack tide

2) Approach dock from downcurrent

3) Don't crowd the light

4) Cast upcurrent of sighted fish

5) Cast to dark water outside light

Dock Technique

Lighted docks are largely a sight fishery. When the current is moving, and there is food about, you will see snook facing the current at the periphery of the light halo. Better yet, you may spot snook in the midst of a feeding frenzy, clobbering bait under the light. In that respect, this can be a "sound" fishery, too. You may hear snook popping at a dock 50 yards away before seeing them. During tide changes, you may not see fish at all, or much bait for that matter. But that does not mean the dock does not hold snook. Consider making a few casts with a sinking plug, plastic shrimp, fly or a live shrimp to see if anyone's home. Occasionally, snook will mill about around a dock light even during slack tide, but these fish can be tough to feed with anything but the smallest lures or flies.

When you approach snook at a dock light, do so quietly, and cast from as far as possible so as not to tip them off. Approach from downcurrent so that you can slow the boat to anchor, or hold your position with an electric motor.

From an appreciable distance, you may be treated to the sights and sounds of somersaulting snook blasting small baitfish and shrimp under dock lights. Or, you may only spot minnows or shrimp skipping

Spin anglers do best on dock fish with small jigs, plugs and plastic shrimp. Below, minnow and shrimp flies.

across the water, while snook "sip" them leisurely at the surface. In the absence of bait, you'll see snook stacked like logs, hovering or slowly milling about. In all of the above situations, there is no prospecting involved. The fish are there—now you must present a lure or fly in a convincing manner. If the fish are red-hot, they'll rush to a lure or

fly that plunks right down in their midst. But that may put them off, too. It's better to land your lure upcurrent of the fish and allow the current to "take the food to the table" in a natural manner. You'll quickly discover which retrieve is best—fast, slow, or a more natural drift while just keeping slack out of your line.

Most forage under dock lights is small, so fly fishers enjoy a distinct advantage. Also, fly fishers can fish a streamer through the strike zone, and pick up and recast quickly, whereas an angler with a spin rod must retrieve back to the boat to recast. Small all-white or grey-over-white flashy glass minnow patterns tied on No. 6 to 2 hooks are deadly, and can be impressionistic or realistic. Some nights it does not matter much. But on others, it most definitely does, especially on hard-fished waters. If the water is clear, go with more translucent tying materials and add a set of eyes to that fly. Also, carry some Clouser Minnows with bead chain or extra-small lead eyes to reach snook that are sulking a bit deeper. Small shrimp patterns in tan, white or light green can score when shrimp are present under a light; some realistic burnt mono eye stalks can't hurt. With the shrimp flies, strip with an even, slow retrieve for best results. Consider tying weed guards (in this case, dock guards) to your flies.

Fly rods in the 6- to 9-weight class are ideal for

>PRO TIP

Capt. Scott Cormier

Specialty: Fly fishing, dock lights

Location: Stuart/Ft. Pierce, Florida

Rod: G. Loomis Cross Current, 9-foot 7-weight

Reel: Saltwater, large arbor

Line: Scientific Angler clear sinking Bonefish Taper

Leader: Six feet of 30-pound fluorocarbon

Fly: No. 2 or 4 Polar Fibre Minnow

Docklight snook tend to run well under 10 pounds, so Cormier isn't overly concerned with high-end fancy reels. However, his choice in fly lines is worth more discussion.

"The head of a floating line is thick, so casts a heavy shadow as it unrolls under a light and while lying on the surface," says Cormier. "I find that a clear, intermediate sinking line will spook fewer fish right by the light."

CURRENT

docks, and since the flies are mostly small, you should consider the size of the snook when choosing a rod. Most dock fish are in the 18- to 26-inch class, but 30-plus-inchers certainly can show up. Some fly fishers like short rods—8-footers are great for casting tight loops under docks and offer good fighting leverage. Otherwise, 9-footers are better when you must cast from a distance to spooky fish.

Dock snook are bite tippet shy much of the time, particularly in clear water, so go as light as you can. Twenty-pound-test fluorocarbon or monofilament gets more bites, but if the snook exceed 8 pounds or so, go to 30-pound. Overall leader length can range from 6 to 9 feet, depending on conditions.

Smaller lures are best for dock snook, too. Plastic shrimp are tough to beat in lighter colors. Small jerkbaits work well, as do swimming plugs less than 4 inches long. Again, try to match the hatch as closely as possible. If you prefer to use live bait, live shrimp is usually best. You can freeline them downcurrent to the fish, or toss them on light jigheads or weighted hooks. Some anglers even float them back to a light under a small cork. Small pilchards or finger mullet are deadly, as you can imagine. Spin or casting tackle in the 8- to 12-pound class is suitable for smaller dock snook, but if live-baiting, there's always the chance that a horse will make a grab and end the fight in short order by "reaching the wood."

Dock Fishing Manners

Regardless of how you approach a residential dock, it is very important that you respect it for what it is—someone else's private property. No dock owner will keep his lights on if anglers are constantly pelting his boat and property with sloppy casts, or causing a ruckus just outside their house at night. Never leave your boat and get on a dock to retrieve a lure. Also, do not crowd another boat that is fishing a dock, no matter if you feel they are not fishing it correctly or thoroughly enough. And don't run your outboard too closely as you pass other anglers dock fishing. No one enjoys rocking in your wake.

Above all, do not cast to a dock or light when someone (probably the property owner) is on the dock and has lines in the water. At the same time, the water beneath a dock is public property (except in limited cases such as dredged, deeded residential canals), so don't let an irate or uninformed non-fishing homeowner think they can bully you away from fishing there. As long as you don't touch private property or cause a disturbance, as a sportsman, the law is on your side. In Florida, a dock owner could actually be prosecuted for interfering with your fishing. SB

Bridge Technique

Snook are a structure-loving fish, and what better structure than a hulking bridge? Or even a little bridge over snooky waters? Bridge currents concentrate prey, and the structure provides multiple ambush points. The biggest night snook are most often nabbed at the base of the biggest bridges that cross relatively deeper water, and are close enough to a pass or inlet to have good tidal flow. Snook are often right at the base of a deep piling, hiding in the eddy. Other times, they are right on top. If there is a soft shadow, caused by either the moon or street lights high above a bridge, snook will also linger within a few feet of the shadowline, resting low and watching above for passing prey.

Be aware that snook bites at bridges can be short-lived, and that some bridges fish better on an incomer than a falling tide, or vice versa, or at the tide changes. And just accept that a hot lure or bait one night might not even get a look the next, and plan on experimenting.

Bridge lights cast a shadow-line, an ideal ambush zone for snook. Fish face upcurrent in dark water.

BRIDGE TIPS

1) **Cast up, across current**

2) **Fish surface baits for sighted fish**

3) **Work the water column**

4) **Fish tide changes**

5) **Use adequate tackle**

Snook are often right at the base of a bridge piling, hiding in the eddy.

Lighted causeway catwalks close to the water are ideal for structure-loving snook.

Hit the Rail

The simplest way to fish bridges for snook is from the structure itself. Dedicated bridge anglers figure why hassle with launching a boat, fiddling with anchors, fidgeting with positioning, and late-night boat wash-downs when you can drive to a bridge, tote a rod or two to the rail and fish? Once upon a time Florida anglers simply tied a big, white feather (jig) to a length of 100-pound-test line on a 12-foot-long Calcutta pole. They moved the feather in a figure-8 pattern near the surface to entice gigantic snook.

Bridge snook anglers today are more sophisti-cated, and diversified, and choose among many live baits and lures. Top baits include live mullet in various sizes, either freelined and fished vertically close to the bridge, or pinned to the bottom with a slide sinker or a big jighead passed through the bait's lips. Jumbo live shrimp are excellent and can be freelined or fished in tandem with a Trol Rite or other jighead. Cast the shrimp-jig combo at an angle upcurrent and work it back along the bot-tom, or at mid-depth if that's where the bites occur.

Live ladyfish, or a fresh headed ladyfish are top baits for big snook. And a mullet head soaked on bottom with a slide sinker can take the biggest fish of all. Livebait hooks for finfish should be sized to the bait; 4/0 through 7/0 hooks are standard. Most live-baiters at the bridges wield 15- to 40-pound-class tackle, and rig with long bite leaders of 60- to 100-pound test. The best lures include lipped plugs such as Windcheat-ers, and big jigs, with

Landing your Catch

With such tight snook slot limits in place in Florida, you'll end up catching and releasing undersize and oversize fish. Please do not simply jettison a fish over the rail. Buy a bridge net to not only land fish too big to reel up, but to release them as well. Bridge nets come in various sizes, cost from $15 to $40 and are available at most coastal tackle shops. SB

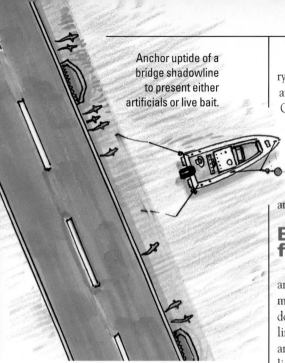

Anchor uptide of a bridge shadowline to present either artificials or live bait.

ryou fish is deserted, you can walk the entire span and walk the jig along without casting at all. Otherwise, cast it at an angle to the shadowline and fish it back to you. Suspending plugs are a top choice when snook are patrolling the shadowline just below the surface. Again, these should be cast upcurrent at an angle to fish along the shadowline.

Bridge Fishing from a Boat

Many anglers prefer to fish from a boat and anchor in a position where a big bait, such as a mullet, pinfish, or jumbo shrimp, can be freelined downtide toward the bridge pilings or the shadowline in the case of a lighted bridge. Artificial lures are presented at a parallel angle along both the light and dark side of the shadowlines. Don't assume snook will be just under the surface looking for prey. Often they will be stacked up deeper, even against the bottom, particularly when there are few baitfish or shrimp or crabs being swept through by the current at the surface. Work the water column by fishing suspending plugs, crankbaits, jigs or deep-diving plugs.

A great way to fish artificial lures or flies is to motor along quietly within casting distance of the shadowline. If live-baiting, you'll usually fare better by anchoring. Rig one rod for freelining and another with a sinker, or perhaps a bare jighead, to get your bait down in the current.

Flare Hawks being a favorite, though plastic-tail or bucktail jigs in the ½- to ¾-ounce sizes do well in lighter current. The Flare Hawk's large-profile skirt "breathes" in the water and does not need much manipulation. Simply drop the jig in, let it reach bottom, and bounce it along. If the bridge

Fly Fishing Bridge Tactics

Though most fly fishers ply the docks, bigger snook prevail under most bridges. Overslot-size snook are commonly caught by fly fishers who break away from the docks, and present bigger flies with bigger rods. This is a boating game primarily, and the key is to cover ground. Rather than casting streamers to the shadowlines and stripping them

Prepare Your Boat for Night Fishing

Night fishing from a boat presents a different set of challenges than day fishing. The potential is always there for an entire reel of blooper videos, or worse. There are a few measures to take to make your night snook fishing go smoothly. Be absolutely sure that your tackle is in working order. Everything is harder to repair at night

Take only what you need. Too many rods or extra tackle bags will get under foot, especially when someone hooks a lunker and you and your crew does an impersonation of the Keystone Cops. Keep all safety gear and ample lights within reach, but stowed securely. Throw a piece of carpeting on the deck—it will cover some of the cleats, latches and other things that tend to reach up and grab a fly line, or trip you up. As stealth can be a major factor, the carpet will also muffle footsteps and dropped lures. On a still summer night, a dropped lure will sound like a cannon against a hard boat deck. SB

back with the current, try this technique to show the fish the fly longer: Position your boat with an electric motor at the speed that keeps you stationary upcurrent of the shadowline, or bridge abutments if under an unlighted bridge. Cast your fly at an angle and then crawl it along with short, even strips. On especially strong tide nights, you can practically hold the fly line, and your fly will

This snook ambushed a bait beneath a lighted bridge fender.

move along a shadowline on its own as the bow in your line is pulled downcurrent until straight downcurrent of your position. Snook have no qualms about belting a baitfish that appears to be struggling to swim against the current to "get out of Dodge." Usually, the strike is sudden and solid, and you do not even have a reason to strip-strike. Just get a bend in the rod once the hook is set, and concentrate on clearing loose line to the reel if the fish is big enough to get onto the reel.

The ideal outfit for this is a 9- or 10-weight rod. A large-arbor reel will help you pick up line quickly. A clear intermediate sinking line gets your fly just under the surface, and will not form a belly as a floating line can when casting across current. For deep fish, carry an outfit with a fast sinking line, or a spare spool for a quick switch.

Top flies for this work include bushy 4- to 7-inch Deceivers, rab-bit strip Muddlers and Sea-Ducers. All-white or green-over-white streamers are standard, but bushy shrimp patterns may save the night, especially during shrimp runs. Short leaders suffice with sinking lines. Even a "homeboy" leader (a straight piece of 30- to 50-pound fluorocarbon or mono) will do. Or tie in a class tippet if you insist. SB

SAFETY
Comes First

Any discussion of night fishing should include personal safety. The chance of hooking yourself or your buddy increases exponentially after dark. Bring reliable light sources, both handheld and signaling. Constantly check your running lights. If the area is devoid of boats, you might be tempted to turn off your navigation lights, but consider that the law requires an all-round white light at anchor, or stern and starboard and port running lights if underway and making way, which you are if electric motoring. Also, your lights let others know that the dock is already being fished. If you are in a paddle craft, you are required to have the ability to display a light, such as a flashlight. Consider clear safety goggles while running or while fly casting. Closed-toe boating shoes prevent you from getting stuck by lure hooks or sharp spines of any snook that slip out of your grasp on the deck. SB

CHAPTER 14

Trophy Snook

On the subject of trophy snook, criteria has to be established. While a 10-plus-pounder should make any fly fisher's day (or night), it would take a 30-pounder or better to excite a dedicated live-baiter soaking foot-long mullet under a bridge or in an inlet.

The very term "trophy" begs for clarification; in the U.S., snook are managed according to a strategy which preserves the largest breeding fish. That means fish of a specific length must be released. Your "trophy" is not hanging on the wall or filleted for the fryer. Instead the trophy snooker hopes to take home a vivid memory, perhaps a photograph.

Well-documented reports of snook exceeding 60 or 70 pounds exist, but the official world record for common snook stands at 53 pounds, 10 ounces, caught at the mouth of the Parismina River in Costa Rica.

As snook grow to trophy proportions, they do not lose their urge to orient to structure. If anything they gravitate to it more. That's why many are lost during battle.

This qualifies as a trophy snook in the confines of a mangrove-shrouded backcountry bay.

Tackle Up

Big snook eat big baits, and do much

Big snook eat big baits or lures, and big snook do much of their feeding in deep water. Though your favorite shallow grassflat or hidden, winding mangrove creek in the backcountry produces a big snook now and then, the odds of catching a huge snook in such places are definitely long.

As snook grow, they don't lose their urge to orient to structure. If anything, they gravitate to it more. That's why so many are lost during battle. It's not because they break your rod, dump your

Casting and spinning rods in the 12- to 30-pound class are ideal for big snook. Inset, heavy monofilament, poly braid line and fluorocarbon for leaders.

spool or pop your line. In typical close quarters, they reach a bridge piling, bottom rip-rap, or the jetty, and then fray through your fishing line and it's game over. So your first consideration is fishing adequate tackle.

If you were to hook a trophy snook in the surf, you could eventually whip it on light tackle, if you have a bite leader. All the fish can do is run up and down the beach, and most stretches have little structure to foul your line on. But around the best big-snook holes—bridges, big deepwater docks, inlet jetties, coastal spillways, piers, ship turning basins and similar spots—light tackle is simply out of place.

In some places, 15- to 20-pound-class casting and spin tackle is considered trophy snook gear. That same gear would elicit laughter on many bridges and piers where anglers routinely wield rods and reels suited for offshore trolling. Bridge pilings are typically rough and often barnacle-encrusted, and the bottom is often littered with boulders, construction debris, boat wrecks—just picture an underwater junkyard.

Though slot limits in Florida have made targeting trophy snook a tad less popular, some anglers still ache to pull on the big gals. They routinely fish 25- to 40-pound-class boat rods and conventional reels (in some cases big spinning reels) packed with mono or braided line in the 40- to 80-pound-test range. Bite leaders of 60- to 100-pound test are routinely used, primarily with live baits or oversize plugs and flare hawk jigs. Much of this fishing is done at night, so there's not much concern about a snook shying from heavy leaders. With live baits, you could get away with

wire leaders. Keep in mind that wire leader was the only material snook anglers used years ago.

Feed a Big Snook Live Bait

Figuring out how to get a big snook to eat starts with identifying what they prefer to eat. Given Florida's 33-inch and Texas' 28-inch upper-end slot-size law, only a snook biologist is allowed to have a direct look at a really big snook's stomach contents.

Florida Fish and Wildlife Research Institute biologist Jim Whittington says, "Trophy snook

This Florida Gulf coast giant was landed in a river headwater.

> **PRO TIP** Trophy Snook

Capt. Dave Pomerleau
Specialty: Trophy bridge snook

Location: Tampa Bay to Charlotte Harbor

Rod: Heavy 8-foot "bluewater" spinning, 50- to 80-pound class

Reel: Shimano Spheros 14000

Line: 100-pound braid

Leader: 100-pound fluorocarbon

Bait: 12- to 14-inch live mullet

Hook: 18/0 Mustad Ultra Point (J-hook)

Pomerleau fishes at night near big structure such as bridges, seawalls and piers. He prefers long rods with long butt sections (rods with fast taper) that you can wedge under your arm for leverage. He wears fingerless bicycle gloves so that he can palm the spool to add drag when necessary. He also suggests you spend some time in the gym before you test your mettle against his typical quarry.

Fishing big live baits requires hooks in the 6/0 to 8/0 range with high tensile strength.

Ladyfish can be freelined live, or fished in whole condition fresh-dead on bottom. Some anglers swear by ladyfish "plugs" or heads.

tensile strength. Also, you'll need stout tackle and line to set such large hooks with large baits. Many anglers who favor live baits now prefer circle hooks. Once you learn to reel up tight on a fish and not execute a typical hookset, hookup success with circles is excellent. Circle hooks almost always find the corner of a snook's mouth rather than the gullet, gill rakers or even deeper, an important consideration for a snook that you must release.

pretty much eat what smaller snook eat, only bigger, of course. Big mullet (either live or fresh-dead), big blue crabs, live croakers, sand perch, whole ladyfish and silver trout are top-shelf baits and in brackish or fresh water, live tilapia are big-snook candy."

Fishing such live baits requires a big hook, commonly in the 6/0 to 8/0 range, with high

Dead Bait

Big snook don't pay much attention to the expiration date of their food. They are scavengers that will take cutbaits and whole dead baits. Night or day, deep river holes, residential canals, bridge channels and inlets are great places to soak whole ladyfish, mullet "plugs" (headed mullet), big mullet strips or mullet heads on bottom. Sinkers ranging from ½ to 2 ounces are most

Trophy Designation

Among veteran snook fishermen, 40 inches minimum has long been the informal standard for trophy snook. However, FWRI biologist Jim Whittington gives a good argument to up the ante for snook, based on their life cycle and unusual protandric hermaphroditic change from male to female.

"At 40 inches, a snook is probably at least 10 years old, but there are a few males in the population. However, the population at 42 inches is probably all made up of females," says Whittington. "The cutoff for all males to switch to female seems to lie somewhere in between. From a regulatory standpoint, it makes sense to save the true trophy designation for snook over 42 inches." SB

This 30-plus-pound snook took a live mullet fished around a bridge piling.

used, depending on depth and current strength, and whether you are drift-fishing or at anchor. If anchored and fishing live mullet, pinfish, croakers (the choice big-snook bait in some locales) or whitebaits downcurrent, the flow will cause your line to rise. Adequate weight is needed to keep your bait near bottom. A knocker rig (where the egg sinker slides freely to the hookeye) is not as effective as a fishfinder rig (the sliding egg sinker stops at a swivel above the bite leader). The knocker rig does suffice when you soak whole or chunks of ladyfish or mullet, or a mullet head on the bottom, which is a deadly method for trophy snook in passes or back-country river holes.

Artificial Lures

Jigs probably take more trophy snook than all other artificial lures combined. Part of the reason for that is a heavy jig sinks deep fast in strong current, and can be fished effectively in tight quarters. It is the best lure for vertical fishing at a bridge, pier or jetty. The standard big snook jig is a bullet-shape leadhead painted white, red, yellow or chartreuse, dressed with bucktail or nylon. Nylon is standard on the popular flare hawk, a jig that presents a big profile when wet, and does a great job at night, even in dirty water. Nylon skirts have little buoyancy and sink more quickly than natural hair.

Flare hawks are available in most Florida coastal tackle shops, and most snook anglers fish the 1- to 1½-ouncers for big fish. The hooks are 4x strong, in the 6/0 to 8/0 range. This jig is fished tight to the bottom, and it takes an acquired touch to keep it bouncing without hanging up. For optimal sensitivity, fish braided line. Hold the rodtip high when imparting action to help decrease snags. Cast the jig slightly upcurrent, tight to structure, and bounce it as close to the bottom as possible. If you are fishing from a bridge and there is plenty of

room, walk along the rail and bounce the jig along.

Lipped plugs, rattling crankbaits and oversize topwater plugs round out the top big-snook artificial lures. Lipped sinking plugs may be the most utilitarian because they can be cast or trolled.

Flare Hawks are designed for big snook. At top, oversize topwater, diving plugs and swimbaits.

Magnum sizes, from 7 to 10 inches, that imitate mullet are tops and can run from shallow to deep depending primarily on the lip length. Lipped plugs and crankbaits require little operator manipulation. The longer the lip the deeper they dive, particularly when worked across or against the current. And some of these plugs are heavy enough to sink while you pause in the retrieve. Many divers and crankbaits have rattle chambers, and some of the "slab-side" style crankbaits shaped like bunker (menhaden) wobble and give off lots of vibration. The only downside is you have to deal with treble hooks; when that oversize snook inhales one, gill raker and gullet damage is likely. You might consider snipping off one of three prongs, or replacing the treble with a good single hook that does not throw off the lure's balance and action. In some case, big plugs are fitted with comparatively small, light-wire hooks and split rings. Experiment and change them out for bigger, heavy gauge saltwater-grade hooks. Just be sure that the action of the lure is not compromised too much.

end. The water tends to be more shallow than at the foot of the major bridge pilings, so pulling the large plugs at a depth of around 4 feet near the docks, mangroves, or other shoreline structure is a good counterpunch to a deeper lure run down the middle, usually around 8 feet deep. Trolling speed should be as close to a crawl as possible.

Lunkers Abroad

Florida anglers who routinely fish for snook may not give a thought to traveling out of the country for them, but anglers from all over the U.S. target snook abroad. Those heading to Central America for billfish, or the Caribbean for permit or bonefish, might consider adding snook to their fishing itinerary.

Costa Rica is where the current IGFA world record was set. Most trophy snook hunters fish either the northeast Caribbean coast near the mouth of the Rio Colorado, or the central Pacific around Quepos. But snook are taken at all rivermouths on both coasts.

Trolling large jointed plugs or hardbaits is probably the most common method. Some of the biggest

Big snook get darker once they spend time in river headwaters.

Trolling is a time-tested method of dredging up really big snook. Using massive plugs that run very close to the bottom is the traditional method. Major bridges near inlets are the classic trolling sites. For the biggest fish, you need to get the lure near the deepest holes, as tight to the structure as possible. Running parallel to the pilings can be effective, but zigzagging through the pilings will get the lure closer to the structure.

Spillway canals are good for trolling, especially right after the spillway is closed, or during periods when the gates have been opened for weeks on

snook are hooked while searching for tarpon in the rivers and lagoons that dot the Caribbean coast. Plenty of big snook are caught on the surf, using bucktail jigs or cutbait.

Nicaragua anglers troll plugs around the relatively remote Rio San Juan and routinely land fish over 20 pounds, but rumors ripple through towns claiming fish three times that size. The last 80-mile stretch of river, with its many feeder rivers supplying ample forage, is the primary destination for the traveling trophy hunter.

Honduras' Warunta Lagoon offers more than 60 miles of snook water. Letting a crankbait sink for 10 seconds before a slow retrieve away from the mangrove points has shocked plenty of vacationers. Finally, from October through December, in the lagoons and river inlets of Belize's backwaters, fly anglers can follow the mullet and sight fish to huge snook. Then, during the dry season (December through June) fly fishing can be tough as the big snook move into the narrow rivers. That's when trolling big plugs is the go-to method.

Rather than hang this snook from a lip-gripper scale, anglers use a sling to lift the fish from the water to weigh it.

Caribbean fishing expeditions are more or less "resort fishing" trips, and no trip to Central or South America should be taken without some research. Make direct contact with each resort, and if your goal is the snook of a lifetime, you need to specify your plans with the lodge. Ask detailed questions about tackle. Most of their big stuff might be designed for the incredible tarpon fisheries. Sometimes, bringing your own gear is the only option.

Trophy Handling Tips

Big female snook gather in inlets and passes each summer to spawn. These females, and smaller males, are hungry during the spawning season, but also are more susceptible to stress and physical damage from mishandling. A large snook hung vertically from a weighing device such as a lip gripper can suffer injury to the upper spine and internal organs. These heavy fish deserve better than to be dropped on boat decks or bounced off jetty rocks; much better to release them while they're still in the water. Bridge anglers should carry a bridge "hoop" net to lower big snook to the water. Unaccustomed to gravity out of the water, there is risk of physical damage to fish hoisted by the jaw for a photo. If a photo is irresistible, support the body of the fish when lifting her, and make it quick. SB

How to Qualify a Record Snook

Weighing a potential International Game Fish Association (IGFA) world record snook in Florida is complicated due to slot size and closed seasons, and what is now considered "possession" of a gamefish.

"In Florida, by law you can't take possession of, or transport, an oversized snook at any time of year, and you can't possess or transport a snook of any size during closed seasons," says Jason Schratwieser, IGFA Conservation Director.

"Further complicating the issue is the fact that fish weighed while on a boat will not be considered by IGFA. You must either catch the fish from land, or from a pier or jetty, or be on a flat that is shallow enough for you to jump overboard to weigh it on firm ground."

Since hanging a huge snook from the jaw to weigh it might cause internal injury, Schratwieser suggests weighing the snook in a net (preferably with rubber-coated mesh to preserve the fish's protective slime), and then weighing the net and subtracting the net's weight from the total weight. Or, a sling like those used by tarpon tournaments. Weigh the fish and sling on land, and then subtract sling weight from total weight.

Any scale used to weigh a fish for an IGFA world or line-class record must be checked and certified by a government agency or other qualified and accredited organization every 12 months, or submitted to IGFA for certification with the application. Of course, all other rules and regulations that apply to other world records also apply to snook. Visit www.igfa.org for rules and an application. SB

CHAPTER 15

Snook Hotspots

Fishing holes deserving to be called snook destinations have common characteristics. Among them, warm water, proximity to estuaries, structure and abundant forage. The most popular have convenient boat ramps and access for shorebound anglers, too.

Snook prefer water well above 60 degrees Fahrenheit and spend a portion of their lives in brackish and totally fresh water. The practical northern limit of snook fishing in Florida is roughly New Port Richey on the Gulf coast and Cape Canaveral on the Atlantic coast. Some snook are caught north of this line following mild winters. Freezes tend to knock off the northernmost stragglers. Spring-fed rivers such as Crystal River appear to be all-season refuges north of the freeze line.

The only snook fishery outside Florida in the continental U.S. is southernmost Texas, in the Lower Laguna Madre and adjacent passes and beaches from roughly Port Mansfield south. And there are numerous established tropical snook fisheries, and a few that are just now being developed.

The practical northern limit of snook fishing in Florida is roughly New Port Richey on the Gulf coast and Cape Canaveral on the Atlantic coast.

Above, this may look like a closed-down Tiki bar, but below the waterline, snook are ready to dance, right.

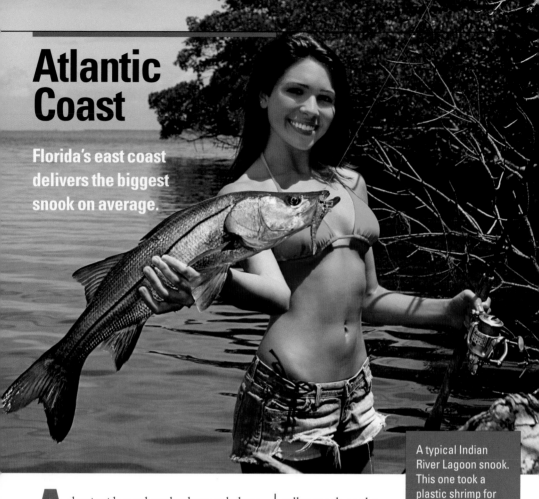

Atlantic Coast

Florida's east coast delivers the biggest snook on average.

A typical Indian River Lagoon snook. This one took a plastic shrimp for this lucky wader.

Atlantic-side snook anglers have a plethora of snook holes to choose from, and arguably the state's biggest snook. Whether you prefer to fish inlets, surf, piers, grassflats along the Intracoastal Waterway, bridges, docks, or spillways, you'll find it here.

Inlets

Summertime inlet fishing on the east coast has long been the sure way to land a big snook. Adult fish group up in ocean inlets to spawn, holding over predictable spots from June through September. Today, a growing number of snook anglers choose not to target spawning aggregations because they feel it's too stressful for the fish . . . or maybe just too easy for the anglers. At any rate, snook harvest is prohibited in Florida waters during the vulnerable summer months. Some anglers limit their summer inlet fishing to single-hook lures or live baits and circle hooks. Biologists tell us snook caught quickly with adequate tackle and handled gently have an excellent chance of recovery.

A word of caution: Navigating and fishing any inlet calls for adept boat handling. Know the tides, the characteristics of the currents, structure and weather conditions. Observe how local snook anglers fish from their boats and follow suit. Don't anchor where others drift-fish, or troll or cut in and out where boats are anchored and fishing for snook. And become thoroughly familiar with an inlet during the day before snook fishing there at night.

The majority of inlet snook are caught deep or on bottom, though bait runs coax them to feed on top. Quite a variety of baits and lures are proven for inlet snook, and it pays to check with local tackle shops for recommendations. Live mullet, croakers, pilchards, thread herring, shrimp, jigs, diving plugs and swimbaits are typically used.

Daytona Beach is basically the "North Pole" of the Florida Atlantic snook fishery, and Ponce Inlet is well within the Arctic Circle. Yet, Ponce is a dependable summer snook spot. The inlet's north jetty is paved with rails; anglers can walk beyond the tee onto rocks at their own risk. The south side of the inlet has a much shorter, unimproved jetty that anglers access from the beach.

Heading south, Port Canaveral anglers enjoy dependable snook fishing around this deep port's docks at night. The water tends to be pretty clear here, because the port is cut off from Banana River waters by locks. Daytime fishing can be tough, thus the popularity of night fishing. Snook find good deep refuge in the Port, deep canals or offshore reefs when winter comes calling. There are also jetties at both the north and south side of the inlet. Port security boating restricted areas are posted at the boat ramps; pay attention.

Sebastian Inlet is regarded as Snook Central, and few inlets get such jetty crowds when snook season is open. Sebastian's north jetty holds tons of snook, targeted both by anglers fishing from this hard-surfaced jetty's rails and in boats drift fishing on both the inlet and the beach side. Live-baiting with croakers and mullet is widely practiced, though jigs and plugs take fish. The adjacent beaches are tops for fall bait run snook, too, though one should avoid times when surfers are catching a good swell. And the A1A Bridge has a catwalk for snook anglers.

Fort Pierce and St. Lucie inlets share the spotlight for Treasure Coast snookers. But only Fort Pierce has a jetty for anglers fishing afoot (the south jetty). The north jetty is treacherous and not suited for foot traffic, so must be fished from a boat. The south jetty has a wide, solid footpath, and paved access and ample parking at South Jetty Park. For boaters, Fort Pierce is fairly wide and

deep. Snook gather along various points on both jetties; the seawalls, docks and rockpiles on the south side are especially productive. St. Lucie Inlet is shallow and subject to shoaling, but its network of barrier jetties holds many thousands of snook in summer. The St. Lucie is primarily a boat fishery,

Florida's Sebastian Inlet north jetty is widely regarded as Snook Central.

A good one heads for the rocks. Inlet jetties hold oversize spawners. Minimal handling is advised, below.

but shore fishermen may access the north jetty by walking approximately one mile south of the public parking lot at Bathtub Beach.

Jupiter Inlet is narrow and busy, with tremendous tidal flows, so it is advisable to fish from a boat at the ends of the jetties, or on the beach sides. The south jetty is paved and has great access and parking at DuBois Park.

The famed Juptier Inlet lighthouse. Jupiter Inlet delivered for this young snook expert, right.

topwater plugs on the beach side of the south jetty, and early birds fishing during the week can even take a few on fly rods. Access is from South Inlet Park, open to the public from sunrise to sunset.

Hillsborough Inlet has hard bottom on the ocean side of the south jetty where snook gather during summer and fall. Surf conditions permitting, anchor inside the right of way. There's no jetty fishing access here.

The south jetty at Port Everglades is accessible via John Lloyd Park. Both sides of the south jetty hold snook. South of the inlet, beaches have both natural and manmade structure that hold snook mainly early in the morning.

Haulover Inlet is known for jumbo snook during the summer and during spring shrimp runs. Boating anglers find night fishing inside the inlet to be most productive.

Miami's Government Cut (Harbor Entrance) is a mega commercial and cruise ship port, and

At Palm Beach Inlet, the south jetty is best for snook, and particularly during the fall bait run. Within the inlet, anglers fish jigs from drifting boats, or anchored up just outside the inlet to cast artificials or soak live baits.

Boynton Inlet is narrow and ripping current makes it tough if not impossible to fish from a boat, although boating anglers stop off the north jetty to catch bait. Anglers on foot fish from both the north and south sides during daylight hours.

At Boca Raton Inlet the south jetty has consistent snook fishing. Parking access is at South Inlet County Park. Early morning fishing is good with

though tarpon fishing gets the headlines in late winter and spring during shrimp runs, snook (and some giants) cruise the jetty edges there. Many snook hang around the many lighted bridges and moorings inside the cut. Deep waters here call for big shrimp pinned to heavy jigheads in winter and spring, or live baitfish such as mullet, pinfish or pilchards on bottom. There's often great fishing along the rocks outside the cut, where you won't have to jockey for positioning in the constant wakes of this busy international shipping channel.

Atlantic inlets hold snook aggregations in the summer. In early fall, the fish feed along adjacent beaches, and by winter, in the upper estuary.

Intracoastal Waterway (ICW)

The Atlantic coast's Intracoastal Waterway (ICW) is a fishy pipeline that runs the length of the state. But for fishable numbers of snook, you should concentrate on the Indian River south of Titusville, where the snook population increases as you progress south all the way to Florida Bay. The ICW has numerous causeways, spoil islands, mangrove shorelines, grassflats, creeks and docks. Some of the best fishing can be expected close to the inlets due to strong current, and particularly during the fall bait run.

Night fishing is a specialty in the ICW, both at lighted bridges and docks, for light-tackle and fly anglers. Some of the biggest snook are hooked by live-baiters at the bridges and along seawalls. ICW docks hold smaller fish, but are good for numbers, even in winter when daytime fishing is tough.

A good flats snook catch from the ICW.

Some years, the ICW sees a more pronounced fall mullet run than the coastal beaches. This much territory can be daunting, but to narrow down your snook search, fish around bait schools—glass minnows, mullet, pilchards and pinfish thrive over the ICW's grassy shallows, and that's where the snook will be. Flats and shorelines inside Sebastian, Fort Pierce, St. Lucie and Jupiter inlets are renowned for snook, and farther south, north Biscayne Bay bridges and residential canals and docks inside of Haulover, Government Cut and Bear Cut hold big snook in numbers, if you don't mind urban-style fishing. Rickenbacker Causeway divides north and south Biscayne Bay, and has produced huge snook over the years, particularly in the wee hours.

The top snook rivers off the ICW include the Sebastian, St. Lucie, and Loxahatchee. The ICW itself in South Biscayne Bay proper is not a snook fishery, but a short boat ride to the mainland shoreline from Snapper Creek south is worthwhile; snook are present along the mangroves, residential canals, and entrance channels to marinas and boat ramps. A few fish reside in the oceanside channels and cuts near Key Largo, Card Sound Bridge (inset) is productive, and farther south, a quick jaunt off the ICW to any Upper and Middle Keys bridge will put you on snook. SB

Titusville

Intracoastal Waterway (ICW)

Sebastian Inlet
Sebastian River

ICW

Ft. Pierce Inlet

St. Lucie River
St. Lucie Inlet

Lake Okeechobee

Loxahatchee River
Jupiter Inlet

ICW

Card Sound Bridge

Key Largo

Florida Bay

ICW

Atlantic Ocean

Haulover
Biscayne Bay North
Government Cut
Rickenbacker Causeway
Biscayne Bay South

Juno Pier, on Juno Beach, is among the top Atlantic snook piers.

Gulf surf anglers alike are blessed with ample public beach accesses. On the Atlantic side, this applies from Miami Beach clear to Canaveral, and on the Gulf, from Marco Island to Honeymoon Island. For snook, some beaches are better than others; those close to inlets, or having features such as hard bottom or rocky outcroppings are tops.

Summertime fishing during the closed season centers around sight fishing "bonefish style" with lures and flies. When the fall bait run commences sometime from September until late October, big

Piers

Vero Pier is the northernmost ocean pier for consistent snook fishing. In Palm Beach County, both Juno and Lake Worth piers have a dedicated snook crowd, and plenty of linesiders fall to live baits and jigs. These two are certainly the best snook piers in the state. Farther south, choose from Deerfield, Pompano, Lauderdale-by-the-Sea, Anglins and Dania piers. Piers are open 24 hours, though Juno closes at sunset in the summer months, returning to 24-hour operation in November. Most piers stock frozen, fresh-dead and live baits, terminal tackle, and some rent gear. Of course, serious snookers bring their own tackle. Call a pier ahead of time for up-to-the-minute fishing reports, but if interested in keeping a pier-caught snook, plan on fishing from September 1 through late October, and again in May. During winter months, most snook leave the coast for inland waters. Be sure to bring a bridge net with you to gently lower and release undersize and oversize, or out-of-season snook that you catch.

Whether you tote a bait bucket or a pocketful of flies, the beach is great for snook.

Beaches

Whether you prefer to tote a bucket of live baits or a shirt pocket stuffed with flies, the beach is a great place for snook. Florida's Atlantic and

plugs, jigs and mullet get the bite. By November, it's best to follow snook into inland waters. When the surf is down, fishing from a boat is possible; when there's a swell, it's safer to fish with your toes in the sand.

Atlantic beaches worthy of special mention include, from north to south, Satellite Beach to Patrick Air Force Base, a stretch with rocky bottom. Sebastian Inlet State Park has a super snook-fishing beach; also consider a handful of other accesses to the north that do not get as crowded. Between Vero Beach and Ft. Pierce Inlet, try the Round Island and Avalon beach accesses, and south of Ft. Pierce Inlet, public accesses at South Jetty Park, Blue Heron, Blind Creek, Walton Rocks (aptly named for its snook-attracting hard bottom) and Herman's Bay. Once you get into Martin County, there are over a half-dozen to choose from, with the stretch Stuart Beach to Bathtub Beach having rocky outcroppings right against the sand. From Bathtub, you can walk the stretch to the north side of St. Lucie Inlet, a great area for sight fishing in late summer.

Hobe Sound public beach is a renowned summer snook area, and you can walk north of the Hobe Sound National Wildlife Refuge as far north as St. Lucie Inlet if you feel adventurous. South of there, Friends of Jupiter Beach, Phipps Ocean Park, Boynton Beach, Pompano Beach and Haulover Beach are good snook producers, but many have lifeguard hours between 9 a.m. and 4 p.m. and no fishing in designated swimming areas. (But if you are serious about surf snook, you should fish early and late anyway.) Other Broward County and all Dade County public beaches are worthwhile, but weekends call for fishermen to be off the sand before 9 a.m. when lifeguards and crowds arrive.

A surf snook gets pulled onto the beach. Most hookups occur right in the trough.

Gulf Coast

Gulf coast passes are snooky highways that lead to grassy, oyster-studded flats.

Gulf coast snookers are blessed with snooky waters—bays, rivers and creeks, oyster bars, bridges, docks, residential docks, you name it. Gulf coast snook may have benefited the most from the inshore net ban of 1995, and stocks have

Gulf coast surf snook are sight fished in summer over sugar-white sand.

rebounded considerably since. Still, severe and recurring red tides can thin the snook population.

Starting just north of Clearwater, Honeymoon Island State Park is a snook hotspot, with spectacular beach and pass fishing, as well as mangrove shorelines, hard-bottom flats fit for wading and even a pier.

Tampa Bay has numerous passes where snook spawn, especially from Sand Key at Cockroach Bay down to the mouth of the Manatee River at Emerson Point. The Sunshine Skyway and Gandy Bridge are just two of the many bridges that anglers can successfully fish from land or boat. Cockroach Bay and Fort DeSoto Park offer some fantastic snook fishing on the grassflats, and most beaches on the outside of the bay are dependable for sum-

mertime catch-and-release sight fishing. During winter, many snook move to the interior of Tampa Bay, specifically rivers such as the Manatee and Little Manatee in south bay, and the Alafia, Palm and Hillsborough in upper Tampa Bay. Fishing methods range from live-baiting in deeper holes with pinfish and mullet where salty, and even shiners and cichlids in the fresh headwaters. Plugs, jigs and trolled crankbaits work, too.

Heading south, the coast is punctuated by many more passes, all of which hold snook from spring through fall. The northern tip of Anna Maria Island has strong current very close to the beach. This stretch has monster snook (along with monster sharks).

Sarasota Bay anglers can choose from many snook fisheries: Casting the shallow grass and oysters along the mainland and Longboat Key bayside shoreline; live-baiting in Longboat, New or Big Sarasota passes; or walking and casting the beaches of Longboat Key. South of there, Venice Inlet is a productive snook pass, and both Casey and Manasota Key beaches offer endless stretches of sightfishing territory. Docklight fishing is a favorite here on summer and fall nights.

Englewood snook fishing centers around Stump Pass and adjacent beaches, or shorelines and bars in Lemon Bay. Just to the south, Charlotte Harbor offers arguably the most varied snook fishing on the entire Florida Gulf coast. "Backcountry" features are numerous, such as winding creeks and tiny bays, island-studded shorelines in Gasparilla Sound, Turtle Bay, Bull Bay, and vast Pine Island Sound and Matlacha Pass to the south. To the north, the Peace River is a top winter snook fishery. With five main passes—Gasparilla, Boca Grande, Captiva, Redfish and Matanzas—Charlotte Harbor has ample tidal exchange and healthy grassflats. The famed Ding Darling preserve, just behind

Sanibel Island, offer paddlers a shot at quiet backcountry-style snook fishing. The waters around Hog's Island, Matlacha and Captiva Rocks can give you a real "backcountry" feel, and dedicated locals are very familiar with plenty of snook holes in each of these areas. The beaches at Sanibel Island might win the award for the most snook per beautiful linear yard. The Caloosahatchee River is a famed winter snook fishery, and some years there are fishable numbers way up in fresh water, to the Ortona lock and beyond.

Estero Bay, like Charlotte Harbor, has numerous grassflats, bars, creeks and shoreline points for snook prospecting; deep creeks on the mainland shore are good in winter. Matanzas, Big Carlos and New passes are the major outlets, and provide good spring through fall snook fishing, as do the adjacent beaches. The atmosphere along this stretch

Many beaches have fallen timber, which is super snook strucutre.

is somewhere between the hustle bustle of the east coast and the glorious solitude of the Everglades.

To the south, Wiggins Pass has long produced snook for live-baiters and jiggers, and the beach at Wiggins State Park is a favorite sightfishing stretch without development. Doctors, Clam and Gordon passes are all close to Naples, and the many residential canals have dock lights that produce all year long.

Once you reach Marco Island, the backcountry opens up, revealing a labyrinth of rivers, creeks, oyster bars and undeveloped mangrove country. From Rookery Bay, behind Keewaydin Island, to Addison Bay behind Marco Island, excellent tidal flow from Little Marco Pass, Big Marco and Caxambas Pass produces good snook fishing. Check out the dock lights and canals around Marco Island at night for fast action.

Florida Gulf Piers

Gulf coast piers tend to be shorter than those on the Atlantic coast, and the water is shallower. Many anglers turn to piers when the surf is too rough for snook fishing in the trough. The Naples Pier is the southernmost structure on the Gulf. The Venice Pier, just north of that, is a bit shorter, but is a good snook producer.

The Sunshine Skyway Pier is actually the old Sunshine Skyway Bridge over Tampa Bay, connecting St. Petersburg with Tampa. There are two piers, north and south, and anglers can drive along and find a spot, park, unpack gear and fish right there. The bridge is lighted at night, a great attraction for snook and tarpon. Continuing north, there's the Rod and Reel Pier at Anna Maria Island, Fort Desoto Fishing Pier, and at Clearwater Beach, Pier 60, which is lighted, open 24 hours from April through October, and noted for its snook fishing. SB

Anglers setting up their gear to fish Fort DeSoto Fishing Pier.

Kayakers at home base for some Cape Sable snook fishing. Inset, snook taken on foot.

Everglades National Park

There may not be a snookier-looking place on Earth than the Everglades backcountry. Here, you will catch snook, or get lost trying. Everglades snook fishing encompasses many styles of fishing

actually, from live-baiting in the passes with boat tackle to fly fishing in the tightest, mangrove-lined creeks of the inside waters. Park waters can be accessed from three general directions: From the north, heading out from the Marco Island area; from the south, crossing Florida Bay from the Keys; or by driving right through the heart of Everglades National Park and launching from the Flamingo outpost to fish either Florida Bay proper, Cape Sable or Whitewater Bay.

Launching at Everglades City or Chokoloskee Island gives you the option of fishing a roughly 30-mile radius that includes numerous mangrove islands, oyster bars and passes at the edge of the Gulf, and a half-dozen winding rivers. The famed Wilderness Waterway is fairly well-marked, but voyaging deep into the Everglades requires careful preparation and good seamanship.

Winter fishing is best on inside waters, clear into the brackish and freshwater territory, where you might catch a snook and a largemouth bass on the same topwater plug. The canal along the Tamiami Trail (U.S. Hwy. 41) is a great winter and springtime fly rodding destination. Drive with one eye on the canal, one on the oncoming traffic, and let the wading birds help you pick your pull-over spots. Tie on a small minnow imitation when the fish are crashing mosquito minnows. Late spring through fall sees snook closer to the Gulf and along the beaches feasting on seasonal baitfish schools.

Figure on Lostmans River, the southern outlet of the Wilderness Waterway, as the southernmost practical destination for a day trip out of Chokoloskee or Everglades City. The Shark River system, south of that, is a shorter trip from Flamingo. The mouth of the Shark is a spigot for vast Whitewater Bay and its numerous smaller bays, rivers and creeks whose headwaters originate in the sawgrass prairies of the Everglades interior. It's all "postcard pretty" snook fishing, but local knowledge is helpful to pinpoint the bite. Classic fishing here is with topwater plugs and flyrod streamers and poppers.

Anglers out of Flamingo pole the mud flats where snook share the bounty with reds and tarpon. When the water is clear enough, snook show well at the edges of potholes. Flies, soft baits and spoons are great offerings. They also stack up in the shallow channels bisecting the flats. And most sand-bottom "moats" ringing the many islands in Florida Bay hold plenty of linesiders, too. To the west of Flamingo, the Cape beaches beckon, and offer super beach fishing. Beach the boat and walk, or cast jigs or soak live baitfish from the boat. Snook peak here in late spring. And don't forget the Keys bridges—snook share the channels year-round with tarpon and permit mainly from Marathon north to Key Largo. They are suckers for a jig, pinfish or live shrimp fished along the pilings.

Texas Snook

Roughly due west of Miami, across the Gulf of Mexico, is the "Little Florida" of snook fishing. But don't assume that Texas snook are small. In fact, before the IGFA began keeping records, the unofficial, but widely accepted world record snook was a 57.2-pounder taken by Louis Rawalt at Padre Island. Texas has seen a once robust snook fishery dwindle to a mere sliver of its former self. Commercial harvest peaked at over 200,000 pounds of snook per annum. After being nearly wiped out, snook seem to be on the rise and a few guides are targeting, and fiercely protecting, the once again fledgling fishery.

The Lower Laguna Madre has all the bells and whistles of the perfect robalo fishery; mangroves, grassflats, barrier island passes, plenty of docks and other structure, and a few deep shipping channels to get the fish through a particularly chilly winter.

A school fish from the Lower Laguna Madre, Texas.

Biologists have not studied Texas snook in depth, as the fish accounts for a very small percentage of the recreational catch. Some believe the population is bolstered by snook sneaking past the border patrol, migrating from Mexico. Regardless, a sense of awareness is growing, and a strict bag limit of one fish, combined with a tight slot of 24 to 28 inches, ensures the present population has a legitimate chance at continued growth. During the winter, the Brownsville Ship Channel likely holds the highest concentration of snook in Texas. The winters are relatively mild, but snook know to keep within a few fin strokes of deep water, so they can be found in or very near the channel most of the winter. Jigs, lipped plugs and soft plastics are effective… when worked in the right spot… at the right time… as long as you "hold your mouth right." SB

Mainland Caribbean

From Mexico to Brazil, various species of snook are available all along the coast. The list of destinations below is by no means exhaustive—every country along the Caribbean coastline has snook prowling its watery border. But some are

A Belize River snook fights for its freedom.

fishier than others, or more receptive to traveling anglers. When traveling out of the country, pre-planning through a resort or travel agency is a safe way to start, but don't allow yourself to be disappointed on the basis of poor planning.

Mexico and Belize (snook, robalo)

Mexico has more tropical coastline than any country in the western hemisphere. On the Pacific coast, black snook are encountered around the tip of the Baja California peninsula, and all points south. Surf fishing is common for these beasts, with the same assortment of lures that fool them in Florida and Texas. Mexico's Caribbean coast has roughly 1,300 miles of snook-compatible habitat, much of it remote. The inlet just south of Rancho Mezquital is probably the first major spawning location south of Texas, and south of that, there's one gigantic estuary after another, separated by rivers and creeks that empty directly into the Gulf of Mexico, Bay of Campeche and Caribbean Sea.

The Yucatan Peninsula, continuing southward

Every country along the Caribbean

into Belize, represents a shift toward clear, white sandy beaches where bonefish take the front page, but snook are known to surprise plenty of anglers. The interior saltwater lakes of the Yucatan Peninsula are among the finest light-tackle snook fisheries anywhere. Farther south, the Belize River is a well-known snook magnet.

Snook might not be the top draw in Cancun, but it's tough to beat the overall package. With plenty of vacation resorts to keep the whole family occupied, the flats and shallows of Cancun offer some spectacular fishing. A catch of multiple snook species can be complemented by bonefish, tarpon, permit, African pompano or seatrout.

Nica-Rica (Caribbean snook, robalo)

Costa Rica and Nicaragua are two of the most famous snook destinations in the world. The Caribbean side of these Central American countries has many "fish camp" resorts, mainly around the

Island Caribbean

Island vacations centered on inshore fishing are not limited to bonefish, permit and tarpon. But don't expect to find snook at every small island; where there's no significant fresh surface water, snook cannot successfully reproduce. Adult fish are surprisingly migratory, and may take up station in unexpected locales, including some of the arid, low-lying islands of The Bahamas archipelago.

Puerto Rico (snook)

With broad, forested highlands and ample rainfall, Puerto Rico has the right mix of freshwater runoff and tropical mangrove habitat. On the populous northern coast, snook are caught consistently in the Torrecilla and San Jose lagoons. Located in San Juan, these lagoons have everything a snook could ever need—vast areas of protected nursery habitat and deep channels at different points around the lagoon. All around Puerto Rico, wherever a river meets the ocean or Caribbean, there will be locals fishing for snook.

coastline has snook prowling its watery border.

rivermouths. Common snook (locally known as Caribbean snook), fat, tarpon and swordspine snook are here in numbers. The famed Colorado River in Costa Rica is just south of the Nicaraguan border. North of that, the Rio San Juan spills into the sea through a tropical web of estuarine heaven. Snook are taken in freshwater lakes more than 100 miles from salt water. The Pacific coast of both countries is loaded with gigantic snook, too. Black snook grow large enough that they command their own record categories, and local scuba divers have talked of spotting snook that would eclipse 80 pounds. Most camps practice catch-and-release fishing. The region's best snook fishing is the run of fat snook, locally known as calba, during the winter.

Panama (snook, robalo)

During the Pliocene Epoch, the land bridge of Panama was created, dividing the Atlantic and Pacific oceans. In an indigenous tongue, the name Panama means "abundance of fish," and today Panama boasts a world-class snook fishery. On the Pacific side, the mouth of the Bayano River in Darien provides the perfect climate for a robust snook population including some real monsters. Gatun Lake, built during the construction of the Panama Canal, is the second-largest manmade lake in the world. Just about every Western hemisphere species of snook has been verified in this lake.

Brazil (snook, camburiacu, camorim)

The Atlantic basin's southernmost snook population is studied almost as intensely as snook in Florida. From different aqua-farming scenarios, to genetic marker studies tracking pollutants in fish, to salinity tolerances in juveniles, fat snook are highly scrutinized. Already farmed in various states within Brazil, the snook farming is likely to expand, with hopes to include the common snook with the many fat snook farms. The southern range of snook is commonly cited to be Rio De Janeiro. SB

The rivers Loiza, Barceloneta and Arecibo are three of the most popular.

Guadeloupe (snook, loubine)

Guadeloupe, a French department, is a collection of eight Antillean archipelago islands that boast a combined 360 miles of coastline. There are snook in Guadeloupe, and a handful of guides who know how to work the water for snook. Locals catch them by hand line or spear gun for the dinner table. On the main island, grassy flats and lagoons are accessible by foot. A few mud and sand flats are accessible by boat, and the channels hold spawning fish, which apparently occurs for a longer period of time than in Florida. Snook are caught in mangrove rivers that resemble a mini Ten Thousand Islands as well. Water temps hover around 80 degrees year-round, so snook can be targeted year-round.

Jamaica (snook)

Honeymoon dilemma: Fish or cut bait? Or plug fish or fly fish? Jamaica gets the press as a romantic spa-resort destination but if you go, don't overlook the line-sided torpedoes in the shallows. With plenty of river estuaries, flats, lagoons and inshore seagrass beds, opportunities for snook, tarpon, barracuda and plenty of other gamefish await. Snook are available all year, especially if you hang around the mouth of rivers like the Ocho Rios. SB

Much of the snooky backwaters of Central America resembles Florida's Everglades.

CHAPTER 16

Conservation

Concern for the Florida snook fishery was expressed as early as the 1930s. In the book "Big Game Angler's Paradise," published in 1937, author Moise Kaplan related anecdotes about his Florida fishing adventures, and lamented that "uncounted pounds of the fish are removed daily," and "extensive searching is required to find these fish."

Consider that this was well before the coastal habitat of South Florida was being developed and populated at a blistering pace, and millions of anglers took to Florida's inshore waters annually.

Clearly, the snook fishery in both Florida and Texas is not as robust as it was prior to WWII, but it is better right now than just a few decades ago, thanks to conservative bag and slot limits, de-commercialization and commercial net limitations. Snook will always be a fragile fishery in the continental U.S. because of this tropical fish's limited range. Habitat loss, severe cold snaps, red tide and water-quality degradation present real and ongoing threats to the snook fishery.

Recreational anglers must continue to lead the conservation battle, and keep an eye on local, state and federal actions that degrade fisheries.

One would think that a gamefish managed by such strict regulations would eventually fall out of favor with anglers. Not so with snook.

See DVD for more about snook conservation.

A snook is held in the current to allow water to rush over its gills before release.

Regulatory Timeline

Anglers should do their utmost to preserve the snook fishery or face more harvest restrictions, if that can be imagined.

Snook were granted gamefish status in Florida in 1957. A glance at the regulatory changes since then makes clear that the state is taking snook conservation seriously. Yet Florida inshore anglers, who have long dealt with ever-tightening regs on harvest, still love to catch snook for sport. An appreciable number release every snook they catch.

Florida anglers can only keep one fish in a narrow slot, and can only do that roughly half of the year. What future regulation may hold is not certain. Anglers should do their utmost to preserve the fishery or face even more restrictions on snook harvest, if that can be imagined. An increase in the bag limit or any other loosening of the regulations would likely depend upon substantial increases in the snook population.

Texas

Texas saw substantial commercial snook landings from the late 1800s to the early 1940s. For example, snook landings at Port Isabel near the Mexican border reached 230,000 pounds in 1928. Since the '40s, commercial landing have dropped with no landings reported after 1961. In 1987,

Good management is key for our snook fishing future.

60 Years of Florida Snook Fishing Regulations

1947—Snook haul seines made illegal in Lee County; in Collier County in 1951.

1953—Minimum size set at 18 inches fork length statewide.

1957—Snook made illegal to buy or sell. Capture by hook and line only. Daily bag limit four fish per day; eight fish possession limit.

1981—Bag limit reduced to two snook per day; two fish possession limit. Minimum size of 26 inches fork length in June and July from 1982-1986.

1982—June and July closed to snook possession.

1983—January and February 1983-1986 closed to snook possession.

1985—January, February, June and July closed permanently to snook possession. August 1985-1986 closed to snook possession. Minimum size increased to 24 inches. Only one fish over 34 inches allowed in 2-fish limit.

1987—Snook regulations now cover all species of snook. August

closed permanently to snook possession. All snook to be landed whole. Use of treble hooks with natural baits outlawed.

1994—Closed winter season now December 15-January 31.

1999—Slot limit is set at 26 inches minimum and 34 inches maximum total length.

2002—Possession limit reduced to one snook per day; May closed to snook possession on Florida Gulf coast only.

2006—Minimum size increase

regulations that limited snook catches to rod and reel only were passed. In 1995, a one fish per person bag limit and a 24- to 28-inch slot limit were established. Fishery sampling conducted by the Texas Parks and Wildlife Department shows that current snook management is effective. Texas fishery managers stress that angler vigilance and the protection of important snook habitat, such as black mangrove, healthy seagrass and estuarine habitat in rivermouths such as the Rio Grande are all vital for the snook's future in southern

Snook stacked up along an inlet jetty during the spawn.

Texas waters. Today, Texas snook account for less than .1 percent of the total recreational snook catch. Most Texas anglers have never actually seen a live, adult snook in Texas waters.

Florida Snook Population Estimates

Today, the Florida Fish and Wildlife Conservation Commission (FWC) estimates that the number of snook over age two in the state is approximately 3 million fish. That's an increase from

the '80s and '90s, but a far cry from what scientists consider adequate to sustain the fishery. A 2006 U.S. Fish & Wildlife Service survey says there were 23,077,000 fishing days in Florida salt waters that year. Ron Taylor, of the Florida Fish and Wildlife Research Institute (FWRI), is steadfast about the effectiveness of tightening snook regulations as the Florida angling population and fishing days grow.

"Raising the minimum size limit, and tightening the keeper slot, directly results in fewer snook

to 27 inches total length; 34-inch maximum not changed. Total length to mean the straight line distance from most forward point of head with mouth closed to the farthest tip of tail compressed (pinched tail).

2007—Atlantic slot changed to 28-inch minimum and 32-inch maximum total length; Gulf, Everglades National Park (ENP) and Monroe County slot changed to 28-inch minimum and 33-inch maximum. Closed season Atlantic changed to December 15-January 31; June, July and August. Closed season

Gulf, ENP and Monroe County December 1-February 28; May, June, July and August. Licensed anglers

must possess a $2 snook stamp to keep a slot snook. In July of 2010 the fee increases to $10. SB

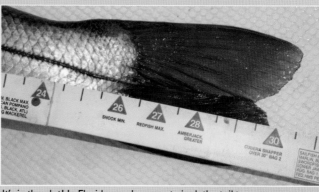

It's in the slot! In Florida, anglers must pinch the tail to measure.

Unfortunately, much prime habitat in Florida for young-of-the-year snook is considered prime real estate for humans as well.

being removed from the population," says Taylor. "It's the fastest way to increase the number of fish, assuming all other variables are constant."

As the population of snook is impacted by loss of habitat, increased fishing pressure, occasional cold kills and red tide kills, there is always the chance of sudden and perhaps long-term decreases in snook numbers.

Habitat

Trying to nail down the relationship between healthy snook stocks and habitat is complicated because snook use such a variety of habitat throughout their lifespan. But after 50 years of research, FWRI scientists have expressed ominous warnings regarding critical snook habitat—the territory required by the young-of-year snook. This would be snook that are about 2 to 8 inches long that have survived through the larval stage but are not sexually mature.

Their habitat includes the fresh headwaters of estuaries, including upper rivers, creeks, canals and lakes that have ample prey (small fish and crustaceans), dense overhanging vegetation for cover from predators and a gradually sloping bank of varying types of soil. Unfortunately, this is prime real estate for humans as well. FWC estimates that over 50 percent of this habitat has been destroyed or developed in Florida, and probably more than that in the highly populated southern half of the state.

Protecting what remains is essential. Most biologists agree that habitat is the prime requirement

Restored habitat in Florida's urban Lake Worth Lagoon. Inset, transplanted red mangroves.

As the snook population is impacted by loss of habitat, sudden and long-term decreases in snook numbers could occur.

for maintaining adequate snook populations— more so than "take regulations" or hatchery programs. In counties such as Palm Beach, where over 90 percent of the natural shoreline of the Lake Worth Lagoon has been developed, residents are realizing the extensive cost of restoring habitat that has seen bulkhead armoring, poorly managed freshwater runoff and discharge, and high concentrations of a variety of pollutants. Restored habitat is not quite as effective as natural habitat, but it's light years ahead of "kind for kind" mitigation, which is the term generally used when habitat is destroyed but made up for by earmarking a habitat that shares few, if any, characteristics of the origi-

nal. Economists are recognizing just how valuable the remaining coastal habitats are, especially in Florida. Left alone, an acre of prime juvenile snook habitat will outperform the most expensive restoration project.

Responsible Angling

There are many ways anglers can lessen the damage to snook that they catch. Tackle choice and careful handling of fish to be released are top concerns.

Heavier tackle, and shortening the battle by whatever means possible, is always better for a released snook. Increasingly, livebait anglers understand that circle hooks not only improve hookup percentages with live or dead bait, but increase release survival because circle hooks result in hookups in the mouth rather than deeper in the fish's gullet. So there's less chance of mortal injury, and removing the hook generally takes less time and handling of the fish out of the water.

Landing devices are better now, too. Rubber-coated nets are widely available and do not as readily rub off a fish's protective slime coating. Lifting large snook by the jaw can potentially damage internal organs or skeletal integrity. When a net isn't

Florida's MOTE Marine Laboratory Snook Hatchery

Recent advancements in snook rearing technology have generated excitement in the scientific community, and anglers will likely reap the benefits. Sarasota Florida's MOTE Marine Laboratory (www.mote.org) has been releasing snook into Sarasota Bay for over a decade, and has made significant strides toward developing an economically viable program.

MOTE is manipulating environmental factors that lead to the onset of snook spawns, and have been successful in making captive snook spawn a full two months ahead of the wild population. Of the 57,000 hatchery raised snook tagged and released into the bay, over 1,600 have been recovered. Estimates suggest hatchery fish comprise somewhere between one and five percent of the snook stocks in Sarasota Bay. The oldest hatchery snook recovered was 8 years old, well into spawning age and possibly contributing to the overall population.

MOTE implemented a release program that includes penning fish for a few days at release sites. This allows for acclimation to habitat and provides protection from predation, significantly increasing survival rates. SB

Young hatchery raised snook prior to tagging and release.

Grasp a snook by its lower lip when reviving. It will chew your thumb as it recovers.

available, unhooking a snook while in the water is the safest method. If a quick photo is taken, lift the fish horizontally while supporting the body. After the fish is unhooked, take the time to revive it until it can swim off under its own power. To do this, grasp the snook's upper or lower jaw firmly so that its mouth remains open, and hold it upright in the current or slowly move the boat forward with your motor. On the flats, pole along to force water over its gills. A snook will actually chew on your thumb as it recovers, and will take off on its own. If you release the fish and it turns sideways, or sinks toward bottom, recapture it and renew your efforts.

Snook are a favorite food of porpoise and sharks, and both have been known to hang around boats waiting for tired fish to be released. Overplayed fish are particularly vulnerable. The practice of chumming known snook haunts with thousands of injured whitebaits is a dinner bell for not only snook, but snook predators. When porpoises have homed in, some anglers take the time to ease the boat close to shoreline cover such as mangroves or shallow water before releasing a snook. Others, when greeted by Flipper, are even more practical and just leave the area to fish for snook elsewhere.

Further, by joining conservation organizations with direct bearing on snook fisheries such as the Snook Foundation (www.snookfoundation.org),

"No snook for you, Flipper!" this angler seems to be saying. Porpoises are known to grab tired, released snook.

Coastal Conservation Association Florida (www.ccaflorida.org) or Coastal Conservation Association Texas (www.ccatexas.org), you directly support research, habitat protection, public education and fisheries management. Membership also links you with like minded anglers to share concerns and ideas. Most local fishing clubs are also very active with conservation projects, and involvement with local habitat issues can be some of the most important, and personally rewarding, activities you can participate in. Finally, the Florida Sportsman Web site and online forum (www.floridasportsman.com) is a great source of conservation and fisheries news and news releases about upcoming conservation fund-raising activities. SB

CHAPTER 17

Cook Your Snook

I f you have had the pleasure of eating snook, it may surprise you that until roughly the '50s, the fish was considered poor table fare. It was then common to cook fish with the skin on, and snook skin produced what many described as a "soapy" taste. Hence, the old nickname, soap fish.

Nowadays, snook rank high as a table fish. Skinning the fillet removes any of the bitterness, and leaves you with firm yet large-flaked white meat that lends well to just about any style of cooking. Snook can be fried, baked, broiled, grilled, poached, and folded into chowders and casseroles.

Florida and Texas snook limits are strict, and when you factor in Florida's lengthy closed seasons, it's understandable that anglers relish a fresh fillet for the table more than ever.

The practice of skinning fish forever erased the snook's old moniker, "soap fish." This firm, mild fish can be prepared in myriad ways.

Snook kabobs are a perfect meal for a crowd. (See the complete recipe on page 200.)

Chill to the Max

In the case of snook, less is definitely more. There's no need to blacken the fillets or add heavy seasonings.

Next to overcooking, "under-icing" can ruin a fresh fish dinner. The golden rule regarding keeping fish is to ice it immediately and thoroughly. And make every effort to clean it promptly once you're off the water (remember that snook must be landed in whole condition).

Don't put your well-chilled fish on the cutting board until your tools are ready to go. A cold, stiff fish is easier to fillet than a warm, soft one. Slapping a cold snook on a sun-baked hot cleaning table at the boat launch and then jawing with onlookers for five minutes about how you caught it will soften the meat. And be sure to choose the right fillet knife—most prefer a narrow, flexible blade in the 6 ½- to 9-inch range. Be sure your knife is well sharpened. A snook won't dull your blade, but a dull blade will massacre your fillets.

Many fish cleaning experts will tell you to rinse the slime from the fish to allow your knife to get a better initial "bite" but once the outer slime is removed, turn the hose off. Fresh tap water will cause the fish to soften, and become dull in appearance. Instead, take the fillets from the fish and set them aside on a cool surface. Dispose of the carcass (in Florida, some tackle shops collect snook carcasses to give to state researchers), rinse the board and dry it before skinning the meat. Put the skinned fillets aside, clean and dry the board again, then trim and/or debone the fish. If you just can't resist rinsing them before moving them off the board for good, pat them dry right away with a paper towel.

Cooking Methods

In the case of snook preparation, less is definitely more. There is no need to blacken the fillets or add heavy seasonings. That would only overpower the delicate white meat. Snook meat lends well to pan-frying, deep-frying, sautéing, baking, grilling and broiling. Just keep in mind that snook is lean, and you may need to add your favorite oil, and baste often if cooking on a hot grill or under the broiler.

Fried Snook Fingers

This is a straightforward way to fry fish. Snook is similar in firmness and leanness to grouper, which is used for popular grouper fingers in restaurants, and frying adds fat which means flavor. The key is to fry small pieces of fish a few at a time, at a constant temp of 350 to 375 F. Always use a coating that sticks, gets crunchy, and does not brown

Long, slender snook fingers cook through quickly without frying too dark or absorbing too much oil.

too quickly. Avoid dark, heavily seasoned bread crumbs—they tend to turn black if you fry a tad too long. Panko, or light-colored crackers such as Saltines, are best for a golden-brown result.

Ingredients

Snook fillets cut into "fingers" approximately 5 inches long and 2 inches wide
2 eggs beaten
1 cup whole milk or light whipping cream
½ cup flour
Seasoned salt and pepper
Panko Japanese bread crumbs or crushed Saltine crackers
Canola or vegetable oil

Slice snook fillets into fingers, moisten with water and season with salt and pepper. Make egg wash by whisking two eggs and either milk or cream until well blended. Spread flour on a piece of wax paper, and do likewise with Panko or crushed Saltine crackers. Dredge snook fingers in flour, shake excess, dip into egg wash until coated. Roll fingers in Panko or cracker crumbs until well coated and set aside for at least ten minutes to allow coating to firm up before frying.

Heat oil on medium heat (if pan frying on stovetop), or calibrate deep fryer until oil reaches 375 F. Dip a tip of a snook finger into oil to see whether it sizzles before immersing it. Fry three to five fingers at a time. Turn pan-fried fingers over after one side is golden-brown. If using deep-fryer, once browned fingers float, they are done. Place fingers on a platter lined with paper towels. Serve with fresh lemon slices, cocktail sauce or tartar sauce if desired.

Snook with Brown Butter and Mashed Broccoli Potatoes

(the author's pick)

Ingredients

2 medium potatoes
Half head of broccoli
1 stick (4 oz.) butter
Salt and pepper

Four 6-ounce snook fillets
6 scallions
Juice of one lemon

This is a quick snook dish with a sauce made from basic ingredients.

Slice potatoes and place in a pot with enough water to cover potatoes by at least one inch. Bring to a boil, and then lower the heat to simmer potatoes until tender. Increase the heat to medium-high, add chopped broccoli florets and cook until tender (no more than 4 minutes). Drain water, and then mash the broccoli and potatoes with 2 tablespoons of butter. Season with salt and pepper, and cover to keep warm.

Season the snook fillets with salt, pepper and olive oil, and sauté in a large skillet over high heat until lightly browned, roughly 3 to 4 minutes per side. In a small skillet, melt the remaining butter (6 tablespoons) over medium heat. Add scallion whites (separated from greens) and cook until butter is lightly browned, about 5 minutes. Remove from the heat and stir in the scallion greens and lemon juice. Season with salt and pepper. Spoon the sauce over the fish and serve with the mashed potatoes.

Grilled Snook Kabobs with Tarragon Butter

(the author's pick)

Ingredients

3 tablespoons olive oil
Grated peel and juice of one lemon
Salt and pepper
1 pound boneless, skinless snook, cut into
  2-inch cubes
2 tomatoes, cored, seeded and cut into
large pieces
¼ jar pitted kalamata olives
1 whole red onion, ¾ cut into large chunks, ¼
  finely chopped
4 tbsps. butter
1 tbsp. finely chopped tarragon

Preheat grill to medium-high. In a shallow dish, whisk the olive oil and lemon juice, and season with salt and pepper. Add the snook cubes, olives, onion chunks and tomatoes and toss gently. In a small saucepan, add the butter and finely chopped onions and cook over medium heat for 6 to 8 minutes, or until the butter foams. Stir in the tarragon and lemon peel. Season with salt and pepper, then cover and remove from heat. Thread snook chunks, olives, tomatoes and onion chunks onto skewers. Grill until snook is cooked through and the onions are tender. Transfer to a large plate and spoon the tarragon butter on top.

Grill snook kabobs until
fish is just done and
onions are tender.

Snook Au Gratin

Ingredients

2-3 lbs. snook fillets
1 can cream soup of
   choice
½ lb. cheddar cheese
1 onion, chopped
2 to 4 jalapeno peppers,
   chopped fine
½ red bell pepper,
   chopped
1 tsp. minced garlic
1 tsp. Worcestershire
   sauce
2 tbsp. butter or olive oil
Seasoned salt
Pepper
Sherry, brandy or white wine to taste

Snook Au Gratin can be served with vegetables, soup or a green salad.

Place fillets in baking dish or large frying pan. Lightly season with salt and pepper. In separate pan, briefly sauté vegetables in butter or olive oil. Melt cheese with vegetables in same pan. Stir in soup and Worcestershire sauce. When thoroughly mixed, remove from heat and stir in liquor. Pour vegetable mixture over fish, and bake at 350 degrees until top browns, or sauté in covered frying pan over low heat.

Quick Snook Bouillabaisse

Ingredients

Two medium or one
   large snook fillet
½ stick butter
1 onion, minced
1 clove garlic, minced
1 bay leaf
2 cloves
1 tsp. salt
½ tsp. black pepper
1 cup fish or chicken
   stock

¼ cup of sherry
1 tbsp. Worcestershire sauce
1 small can tomatoes
1 can shrimp (or fresh shelled)
1 can baby clams

Skin and fillet snook, retaining head, skin and bones. Discard organs.

Boil all parts, except fillets, in enough water to cover for 20 minutes. Strain.

In a large frying pan, sauté onion and garlic and then brown snook fillets. Add all other ingredients and stock and simmer for 15 minutes. SB

Snook is firm enough to hold up to cooking in liquid for chowders or this bouillabaisse.

INDEX

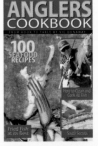

BOOKS Sportsman's Best: Book & DVD Series

The most complete series of how-to books and DVDs in print. Each book in the series has over 200 color photographs and easy-to-follow illustrations. Each book focuses on specific techniques, tackle options and tips from the experts and pros. Average book size 240 pages. **$19.95 Ea.**

Sportsman's Best DVD (only) The editors of *Florida Sportsman* and *Shallow Water Angler* fish with experts from Texas to Maine focusing on techniques that will help you, no matter where you live, catch more fish. Each DVD is professionally shot while fishing on the water. They're made to educate as well as entertain. Approx. length 65 minutes. **$14.95 Ea.**

Fish Book Series by Vic Dunaway

• **Sport Fish of Florida** • **Sport Fish of the Gulf of Mexico**
Sport Fish of the Atlantic • **Sport Fish of Fresh Water** • **Sport Fish of the Pacific**

Beautifully color-illustrated fish identification books. Food values, distinguishing features, average and record sizes, angling methods and more. **$16.95 Ea.**

Many FS/SWA Items also Available at Tackle and Book Stores.

SNOOK DVD

Sportsman's Best: Snook DVD brings the pages of this accompanying book to life. Join author Brett Fitzgerald, the editors of *Florida Sportsman* magazine, and some of Florida's best snook guides, as they explain sure-fire tactics for tackling the formidable linesider. Climb aboard, and we'll cover tides, tackle, structure, conservation and everything in between.

FEATURES

- ► THE SNOOK
- ► TACKLE
- ► CHOOSING THE RIGHT BOAT
- ► BAITS AND LURES
    - JIGS, SOFT PLASTICS, PLUGS AND FLIES
- ► TECHNIQUES
    - READING THE WATER
    - MANMADE STRUCTURE
    - NATURAL STRUCTURE
- ► CONSERVATION

Copyright 2009 by Florida Sportsman www.floridasportsman.com

DVD VIDEO

SPORTSMAN'S BEST SNOOK

If you're looking to find a more exciting in gamefish than snook, good luck. It's go be hard to do. Once hooked, this ga will make surface-clearing jump powerful, heart-stopping ru effort to shake the hook, line on the nearest stru

The best way to expe this amazing fish is to ge water and hook one. If t eluded you, or you've los many snook under docks mangroves, watch this hig nition DVD in the comfort o own home and then put your knowledge to the test. This bo and DVD are a must-have for an snook angler, from novice to expe

—Blair Wickstrom, Publisher

DVD Executive Producer: Paul Farnsworth
DVD Associate Producer: Matt Weinhaus